FESTIVE TRANQUILITY

A Christmas Coloring Book for Adults

CRYSTAL LAKE ENTERTAINMENT

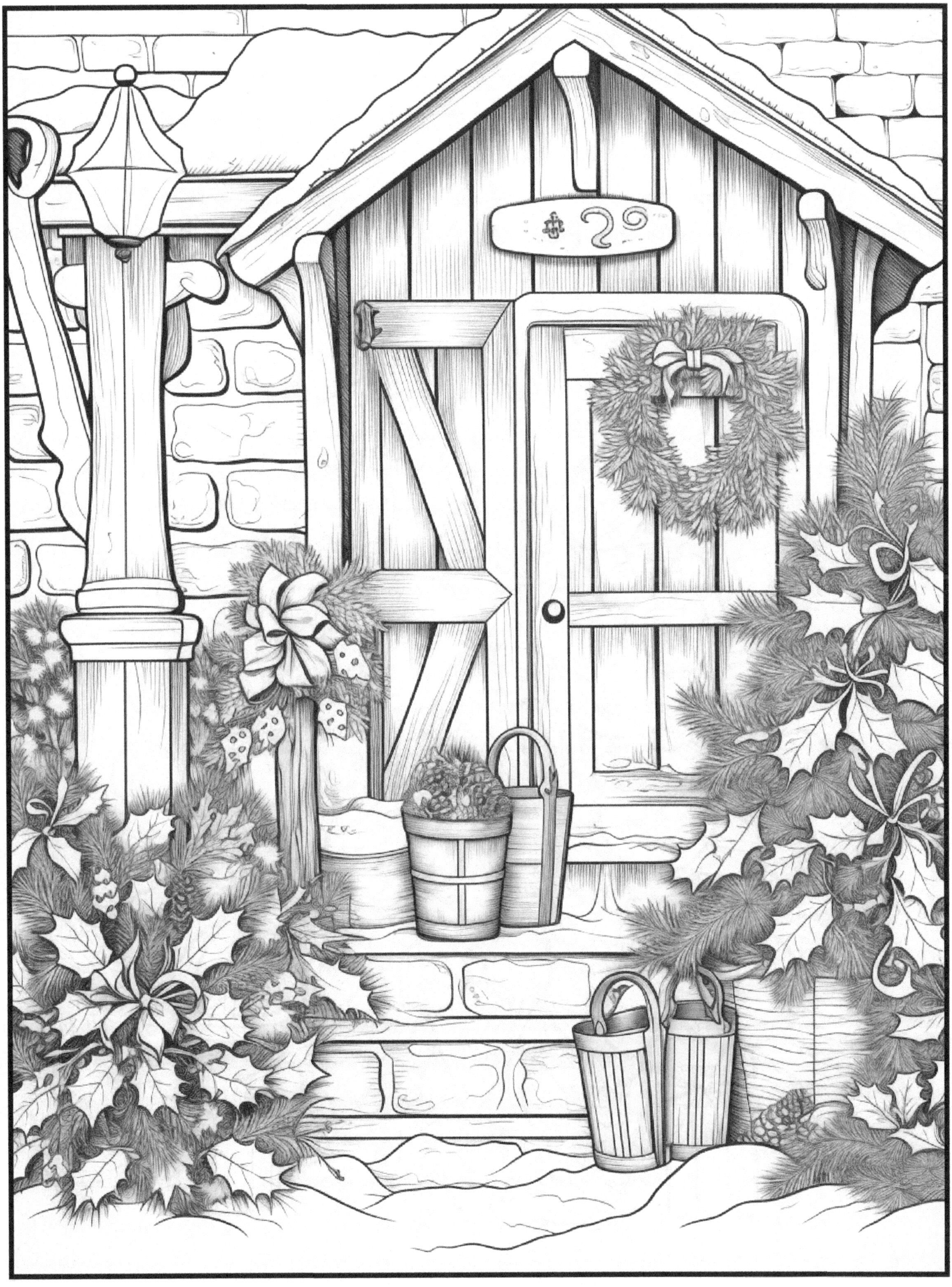

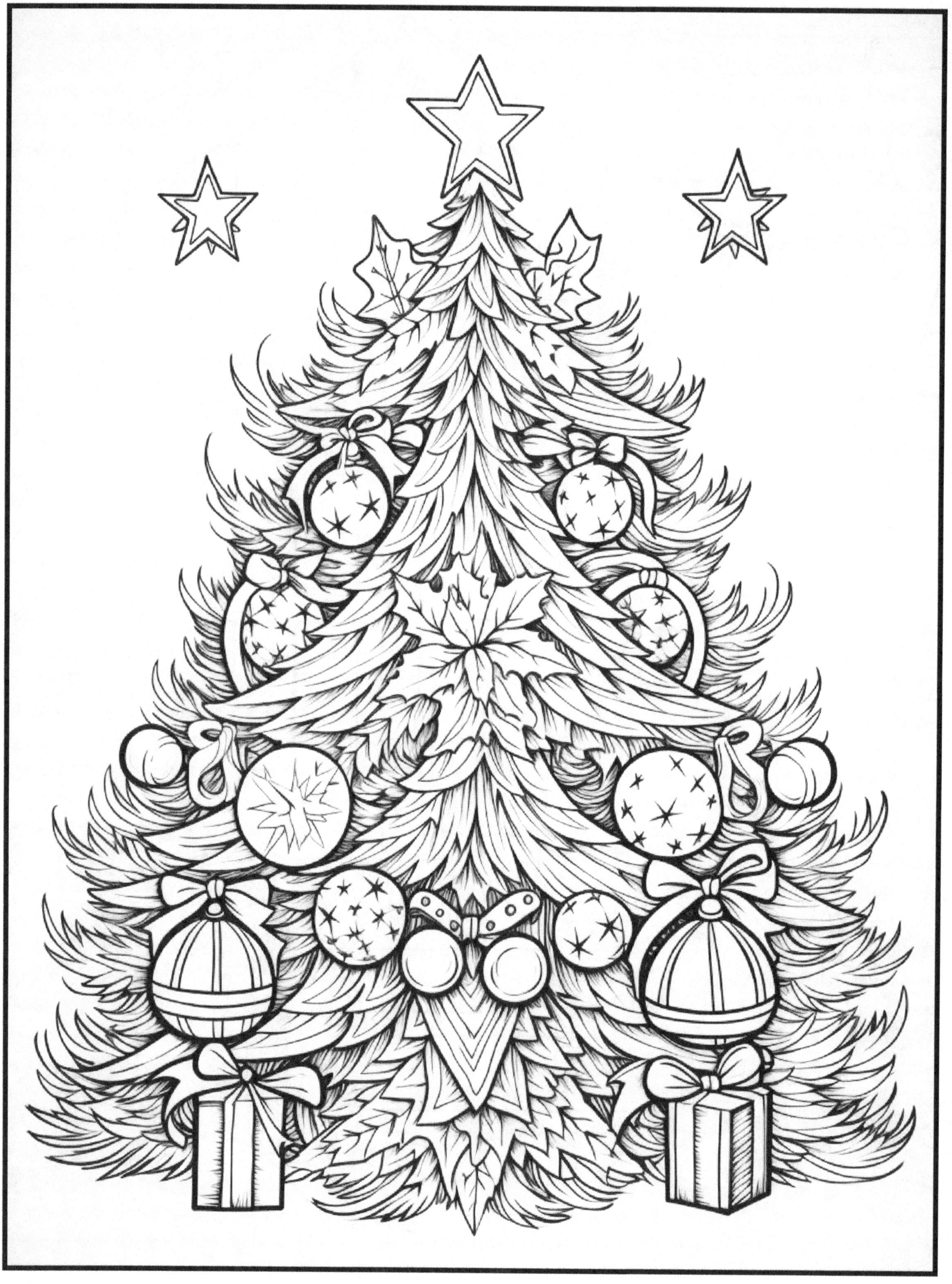

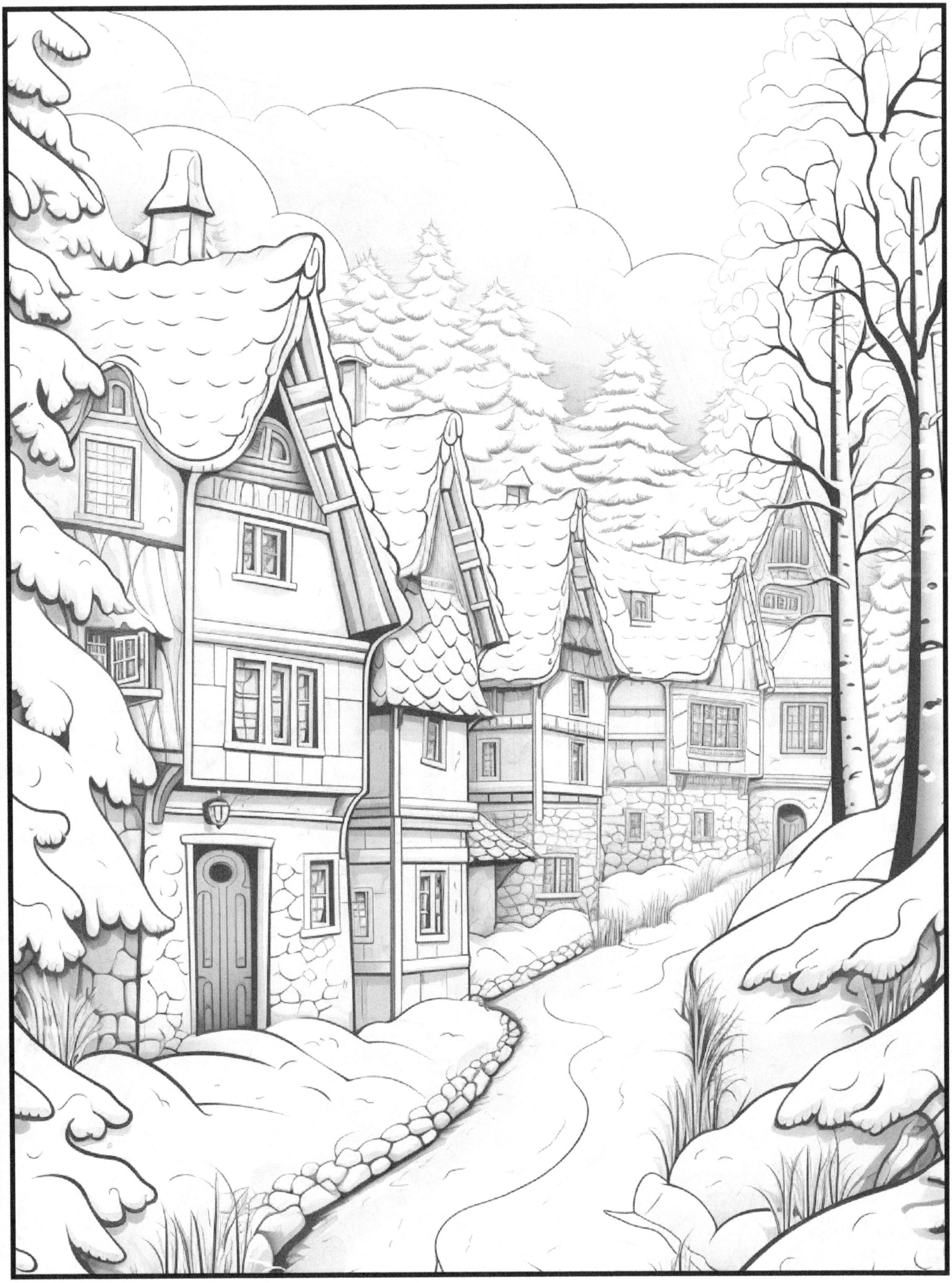

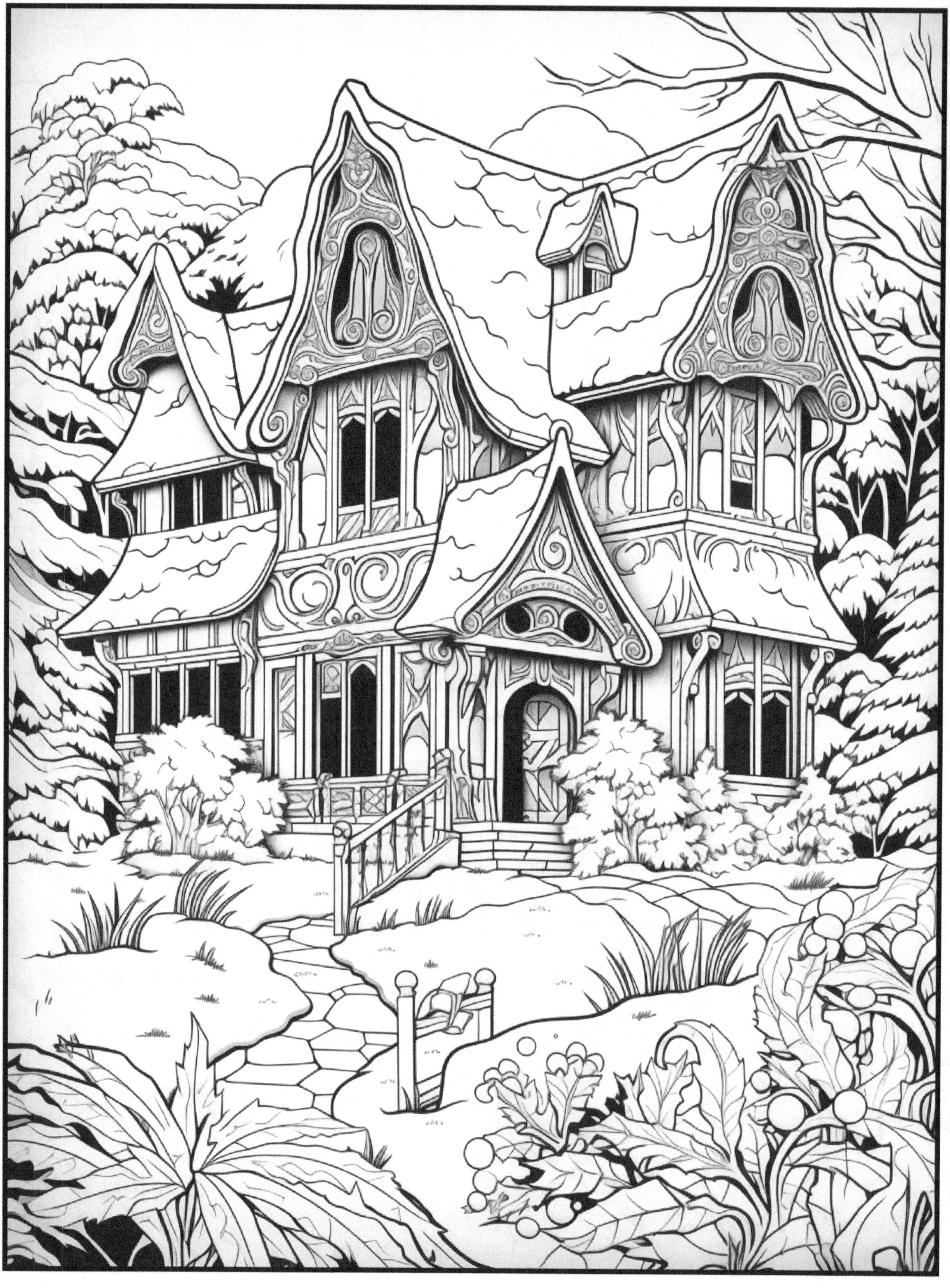

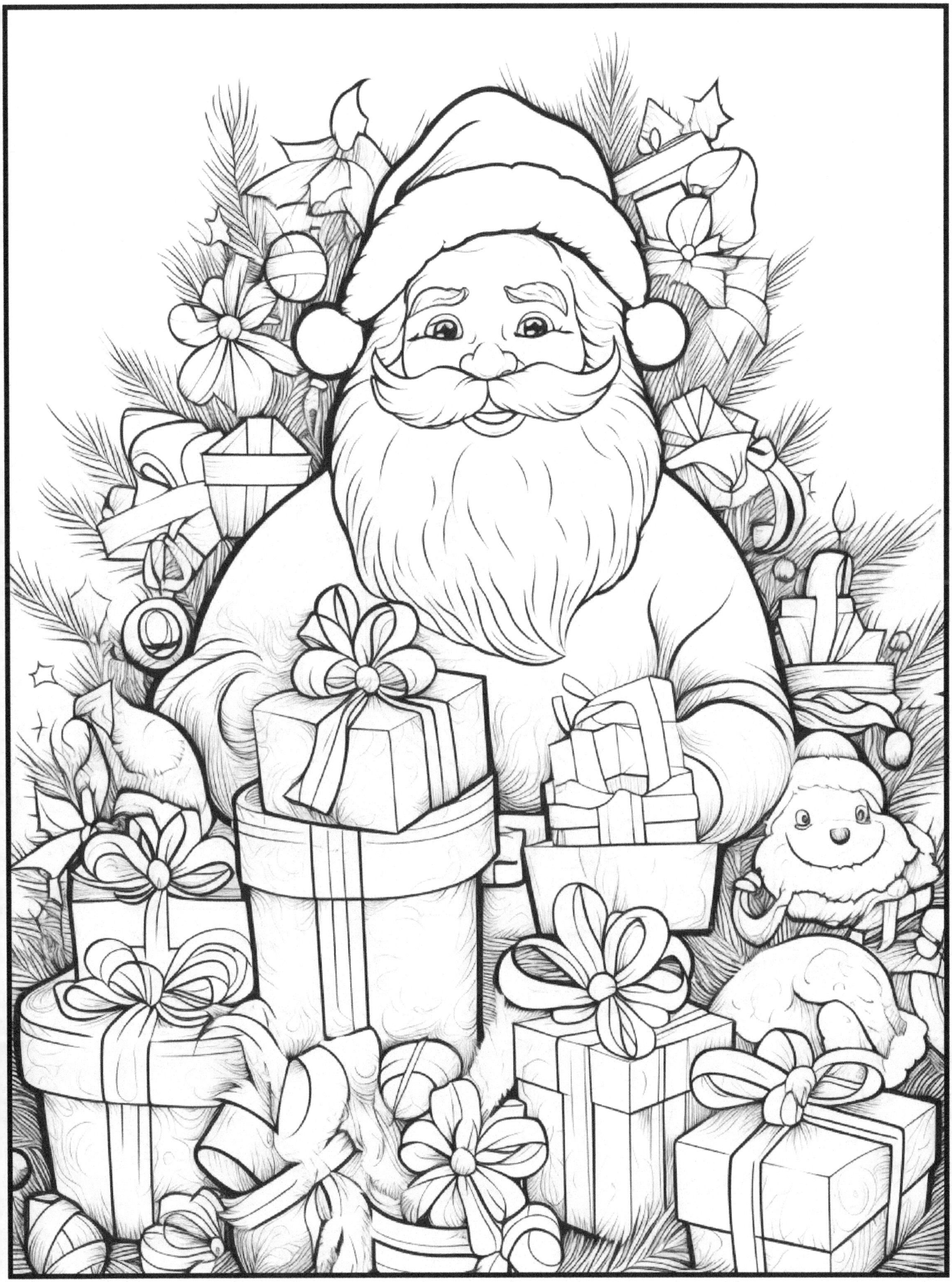

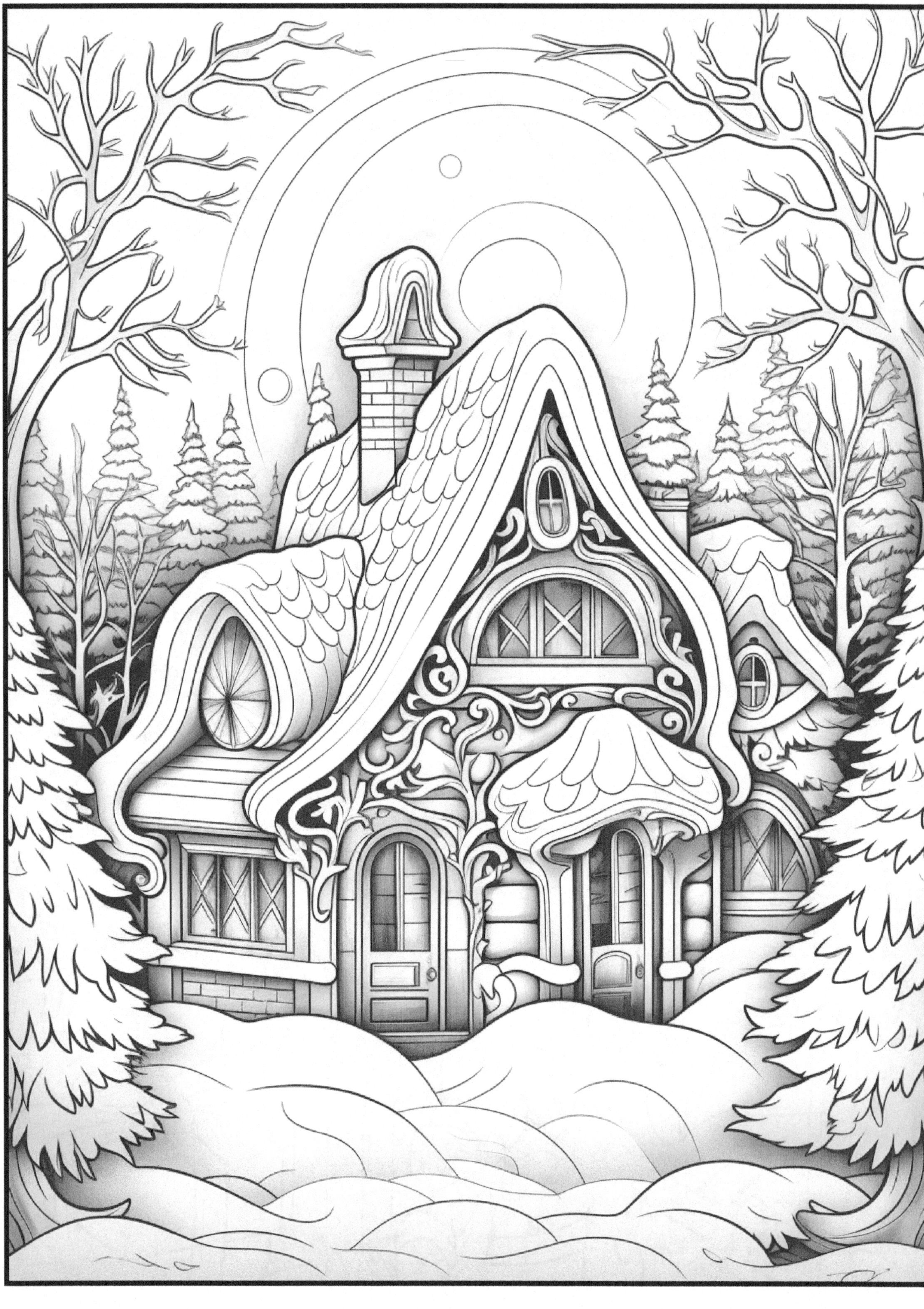

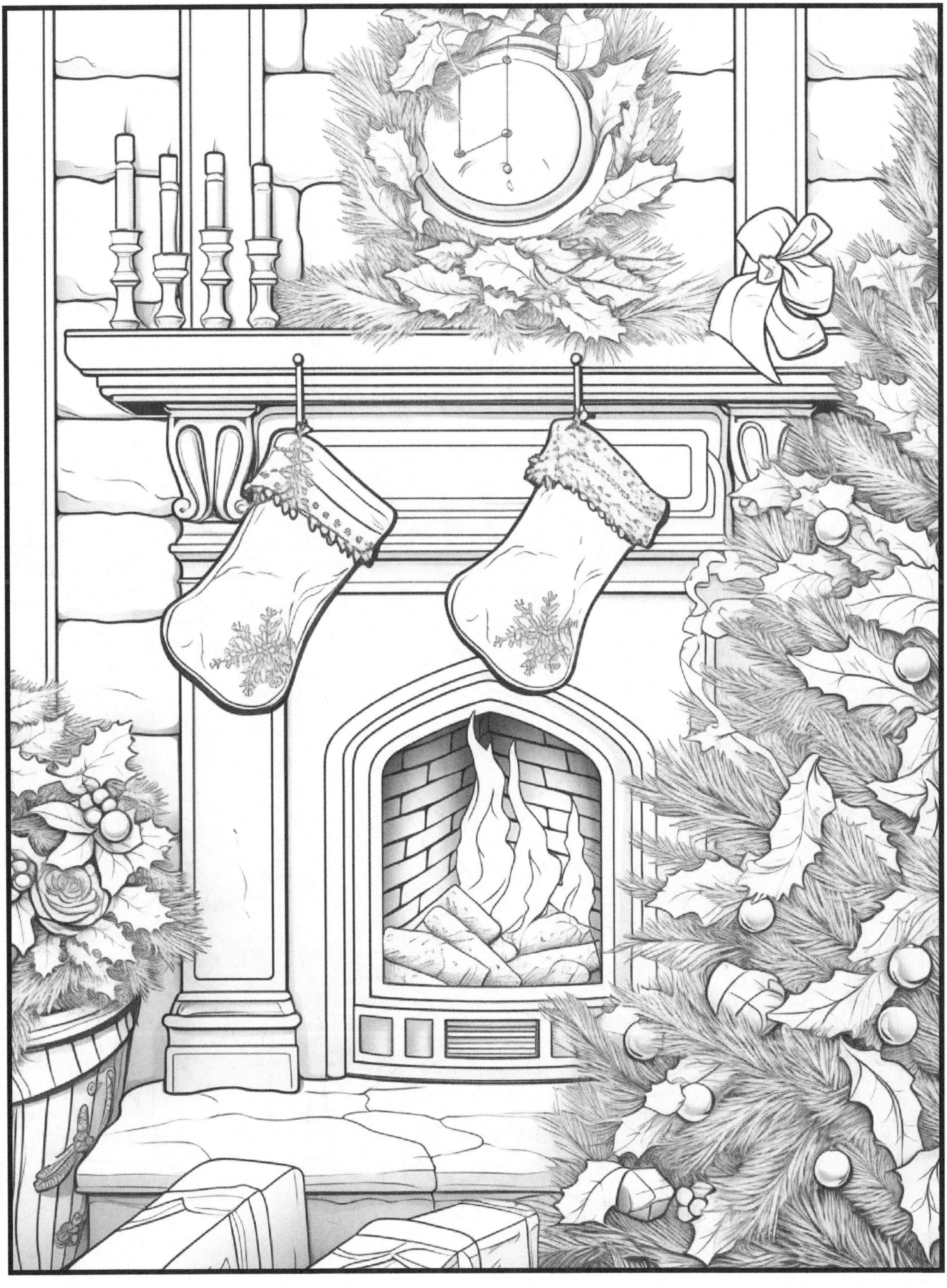

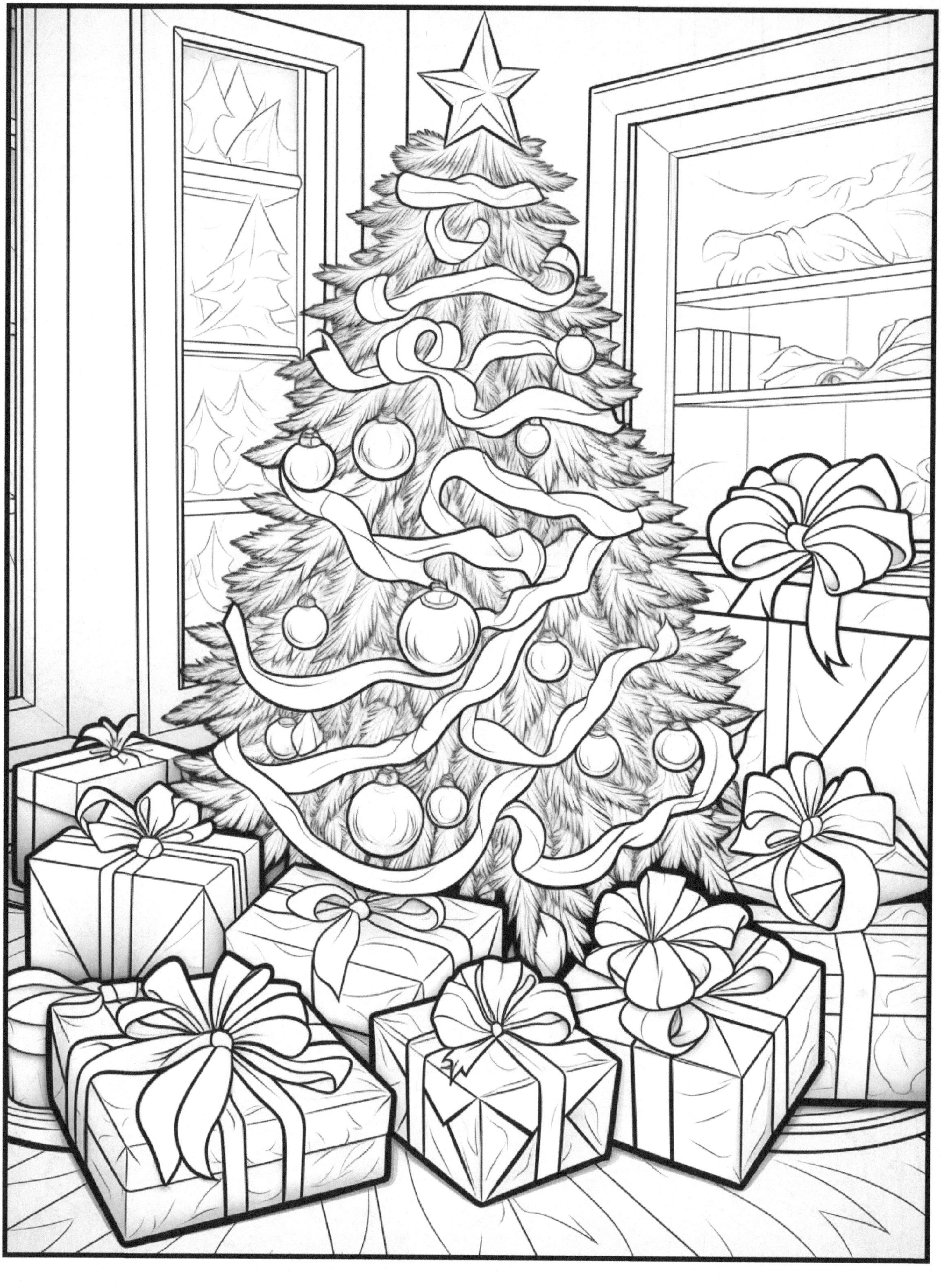

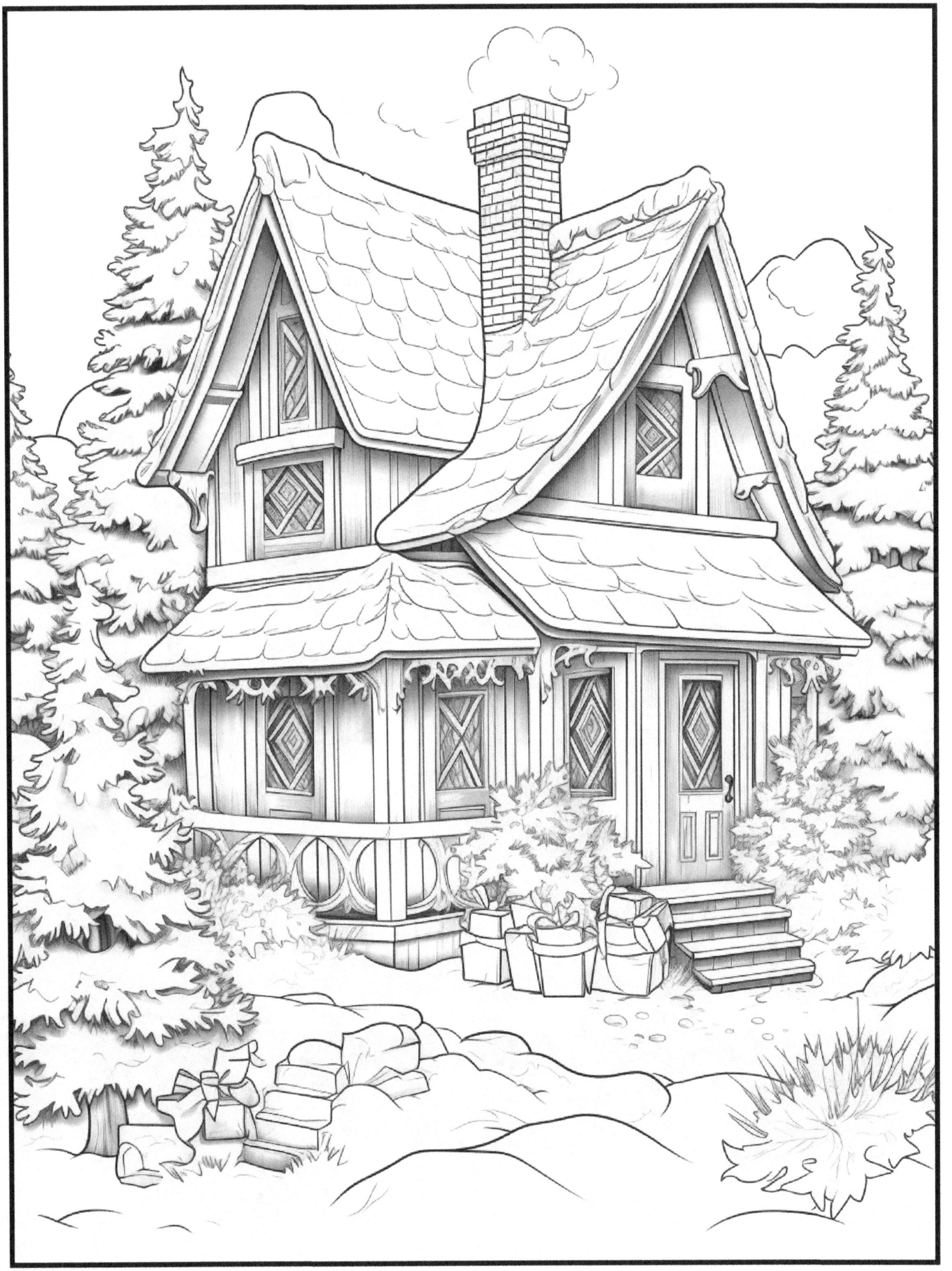

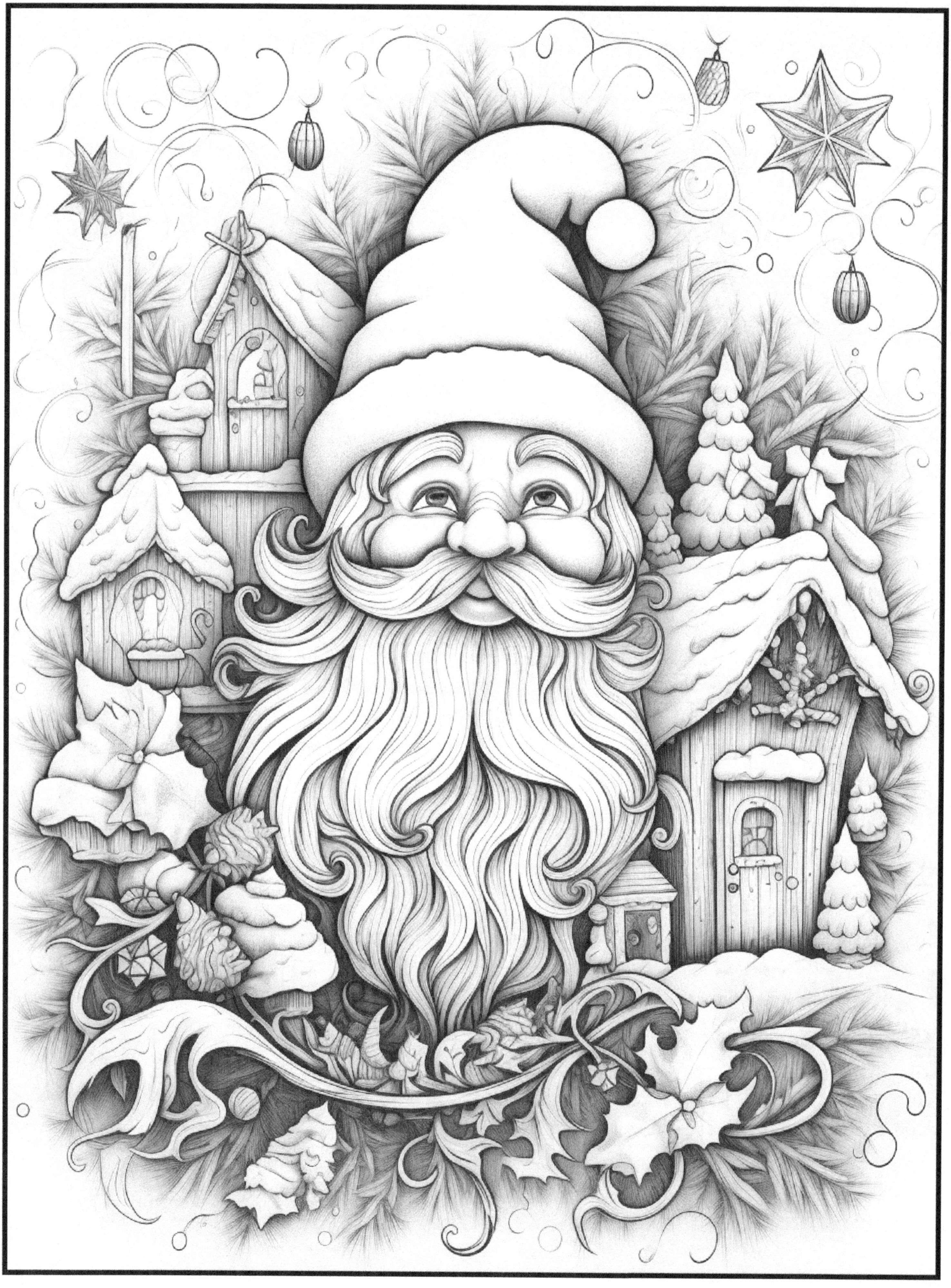

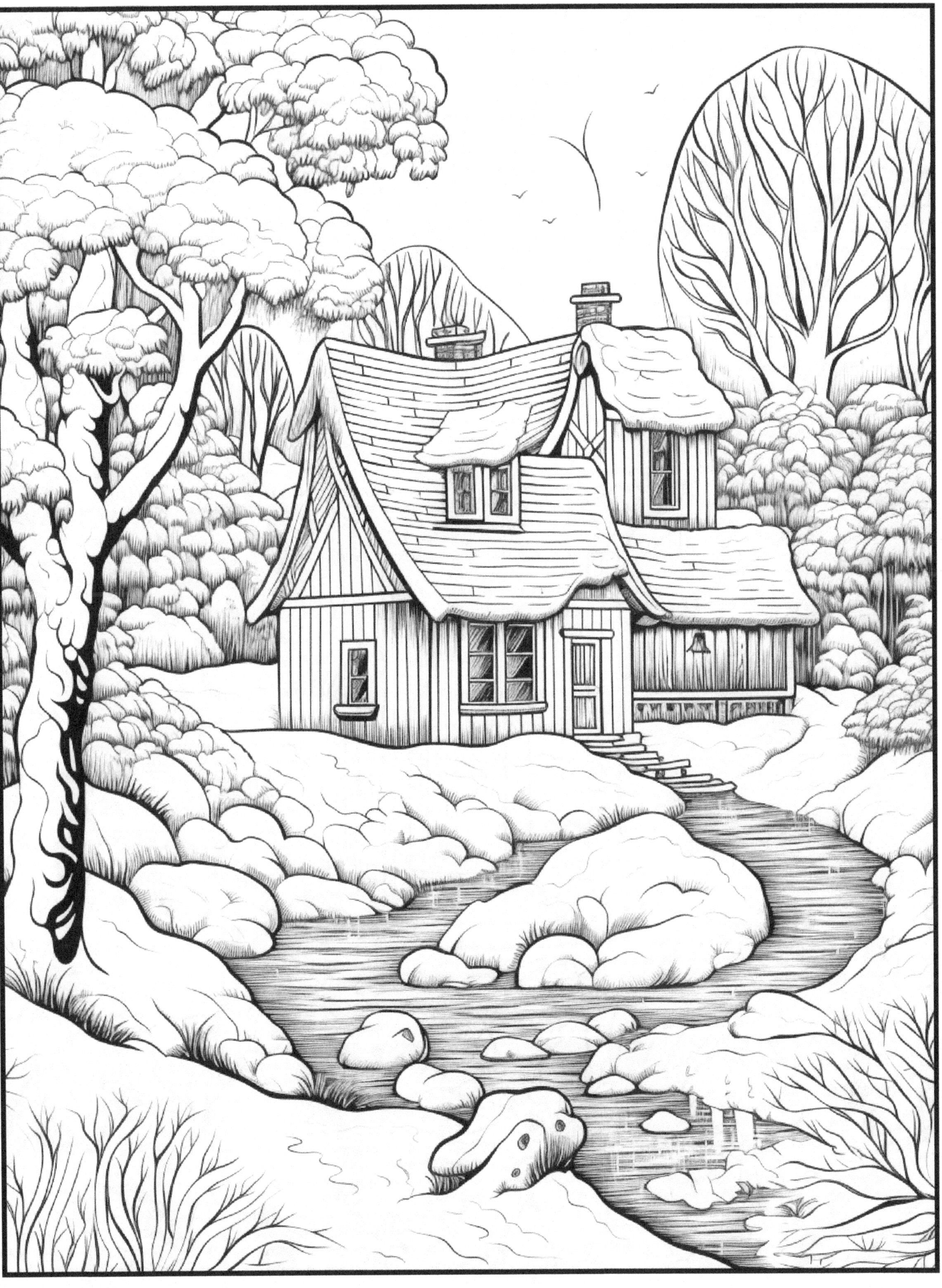

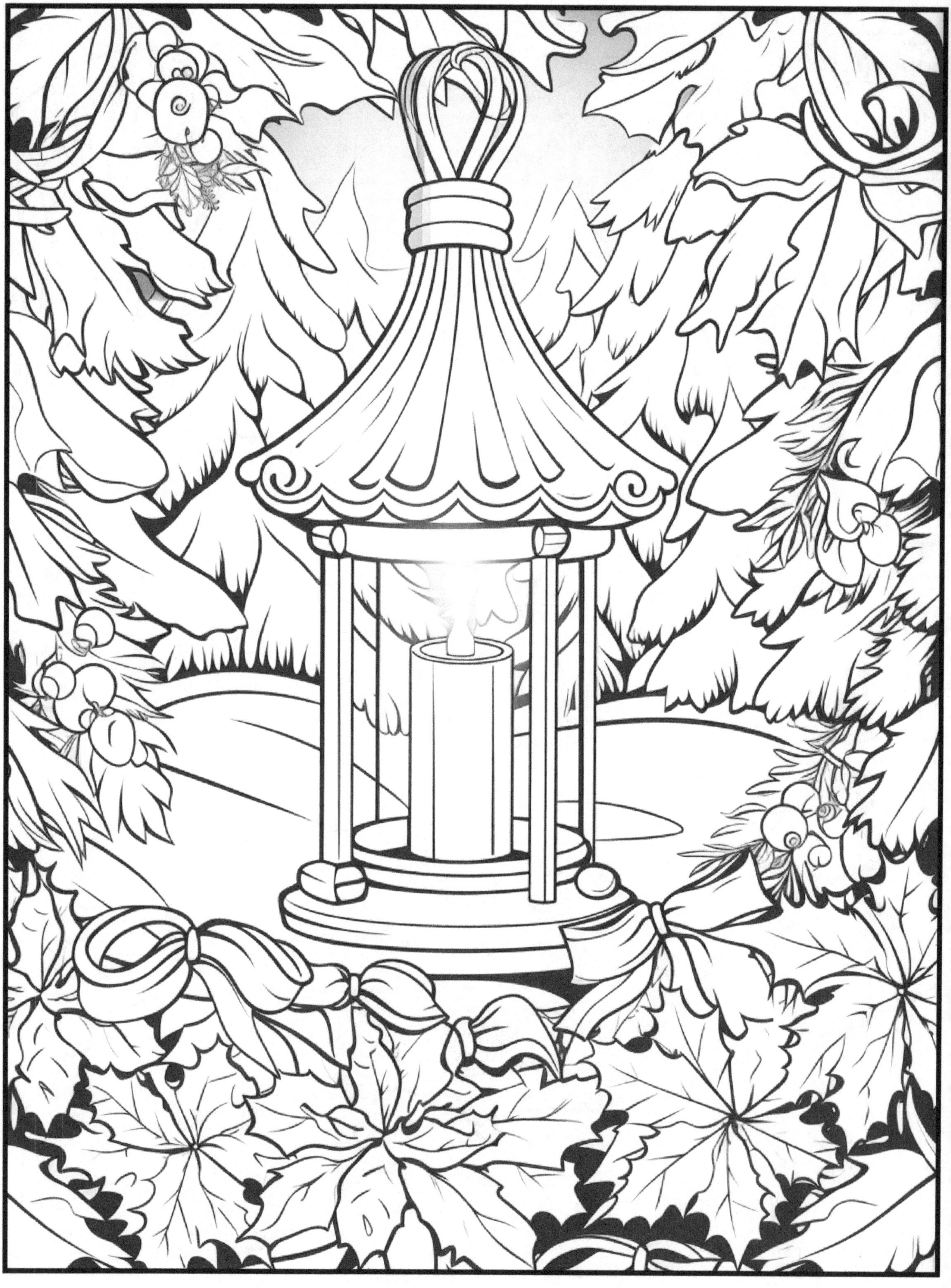

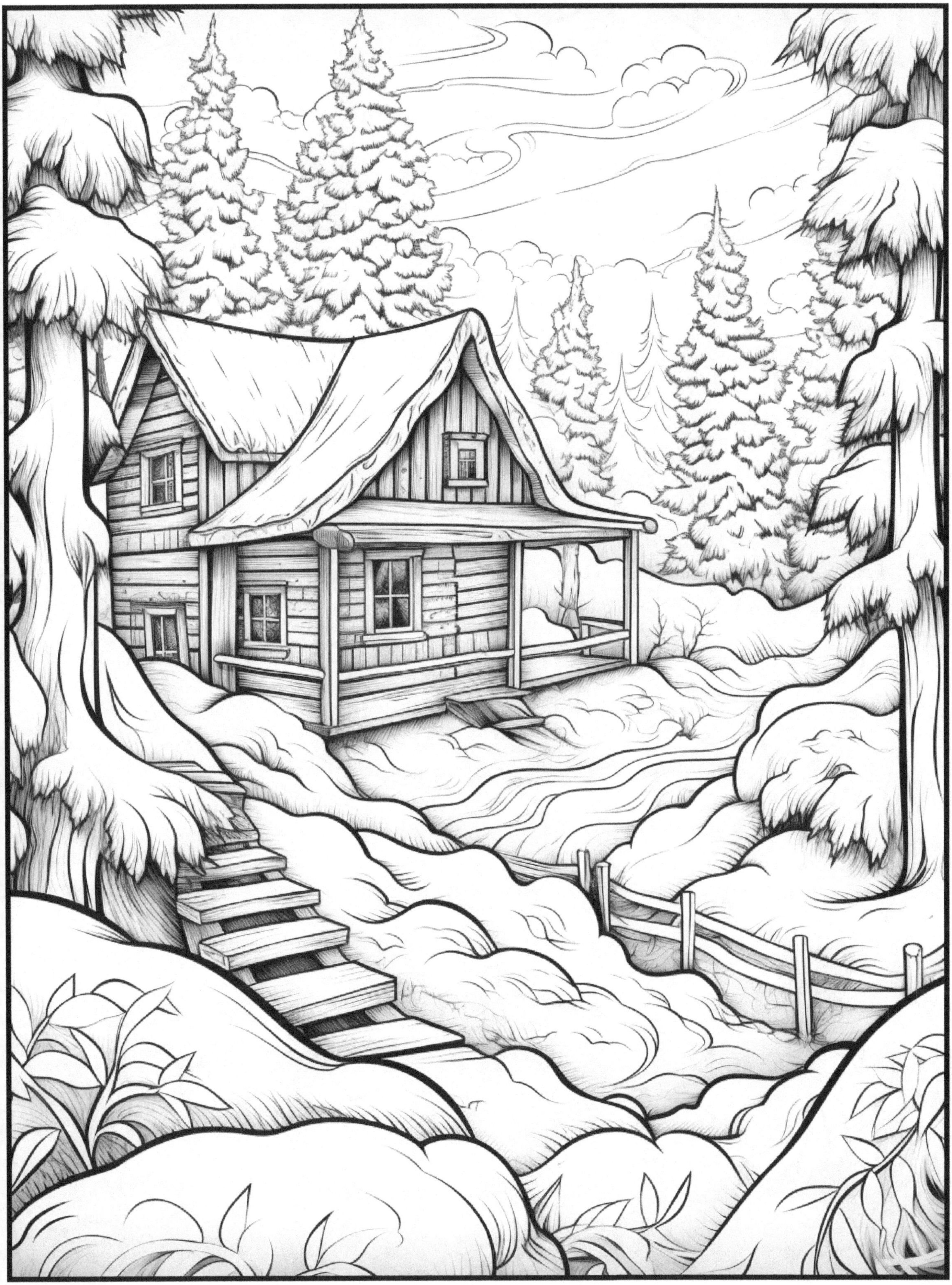

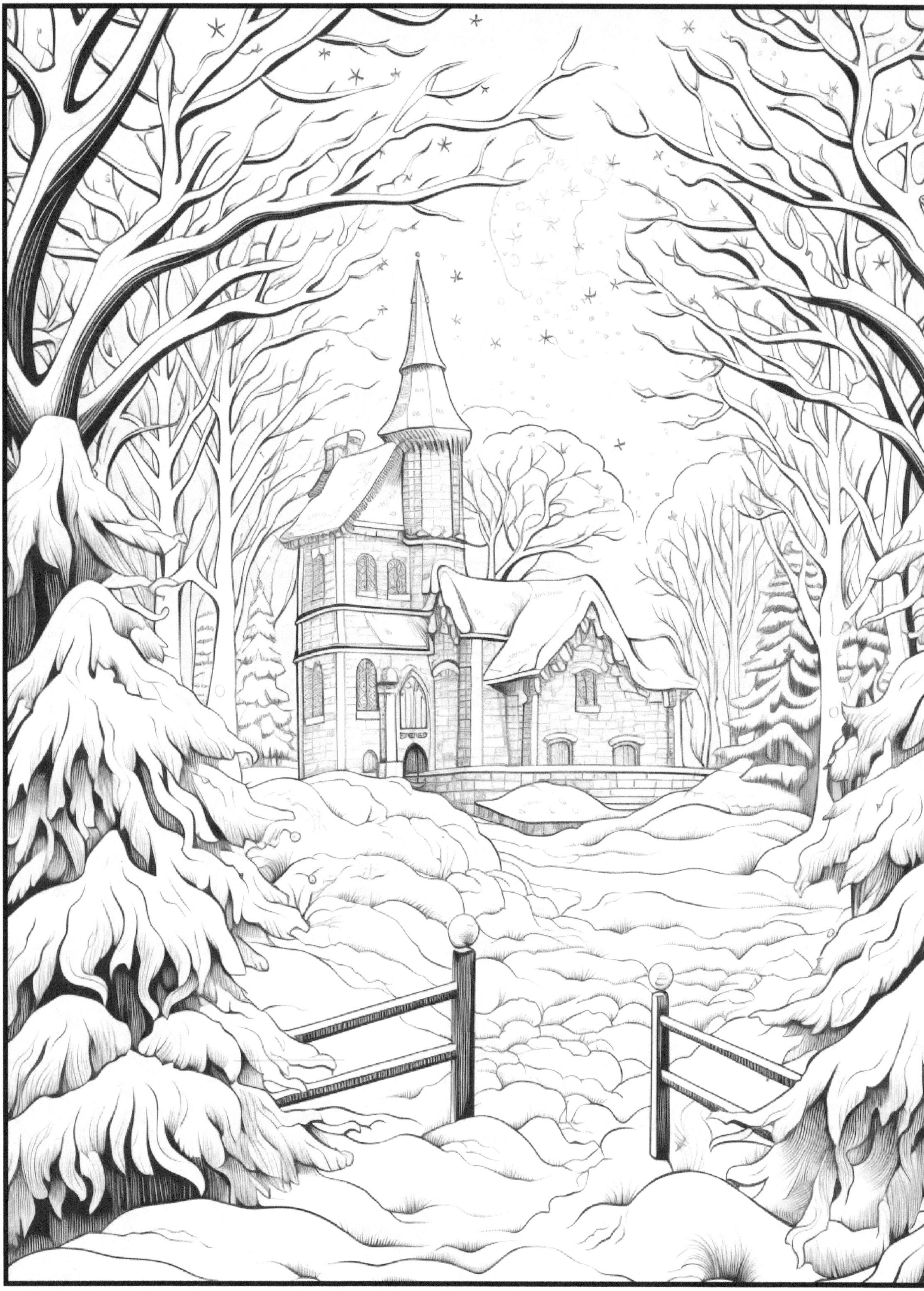

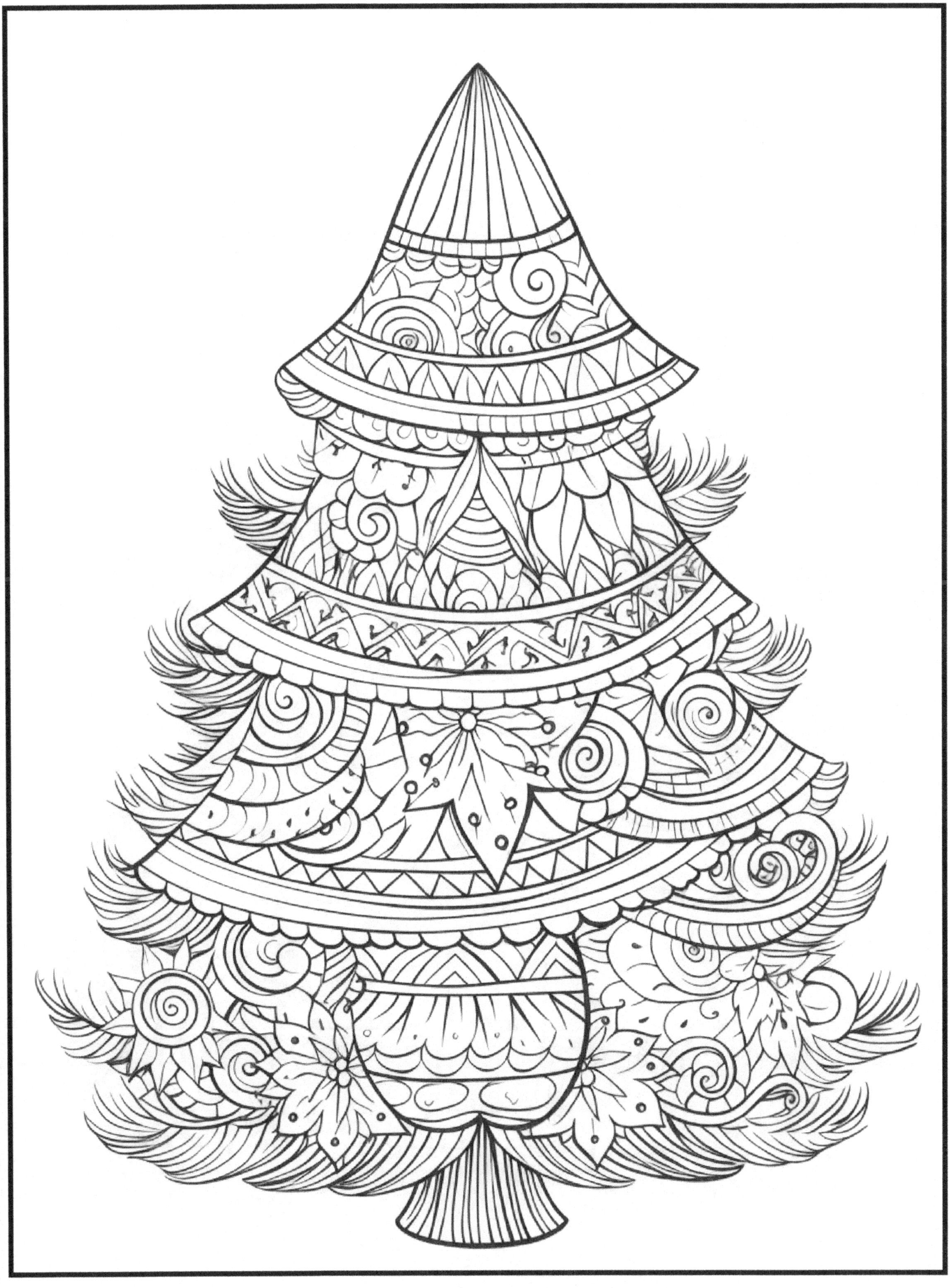

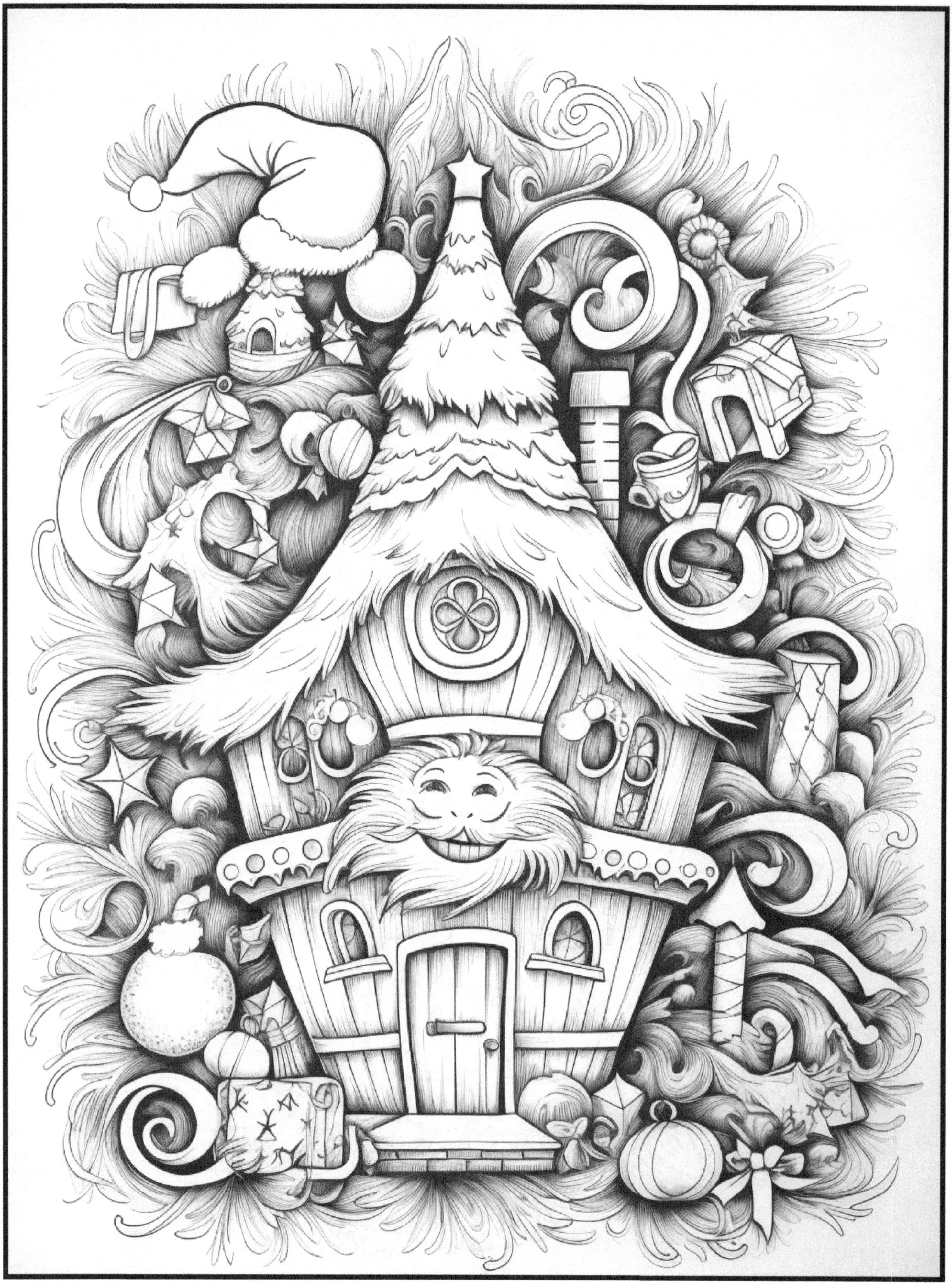

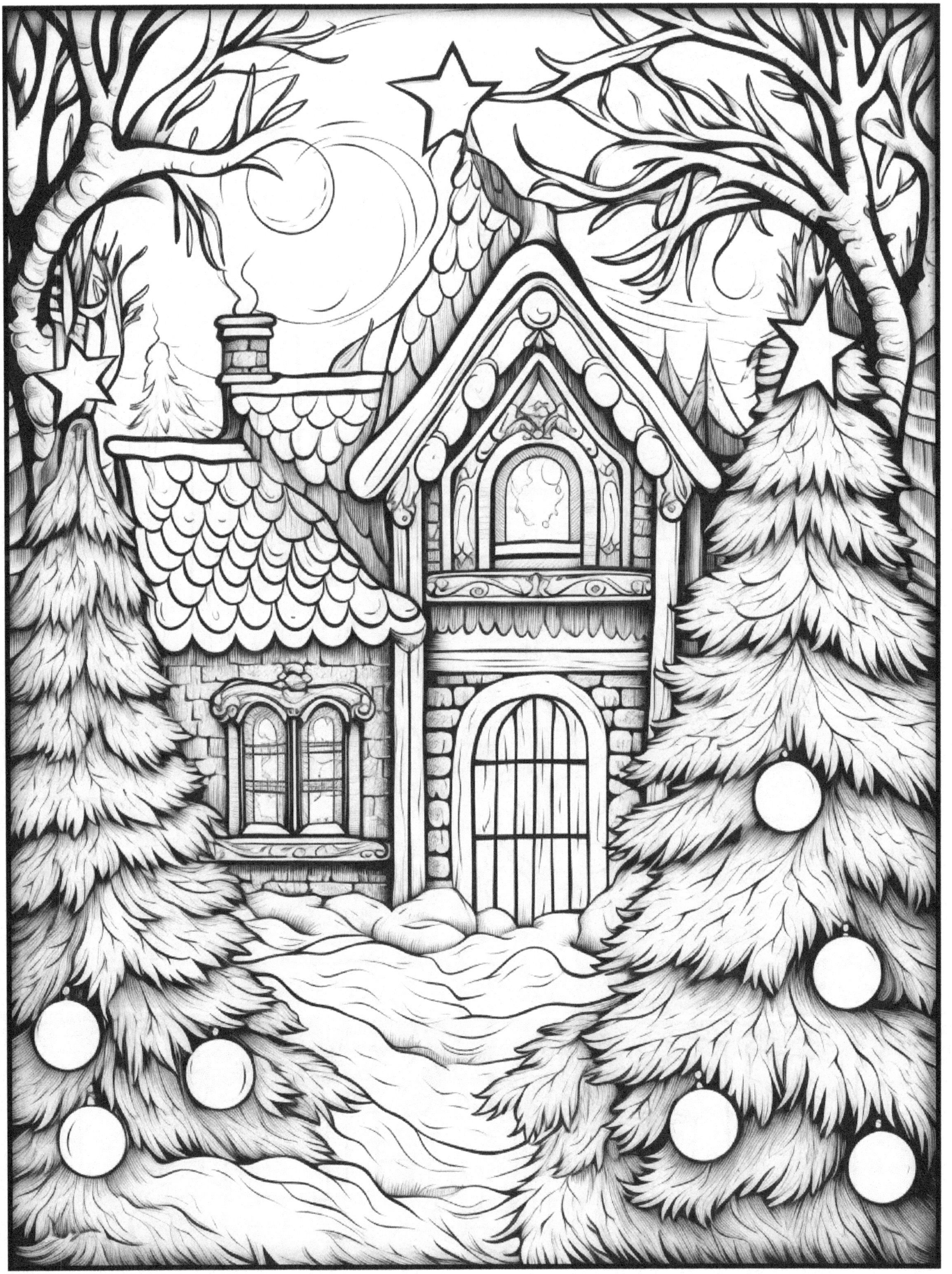

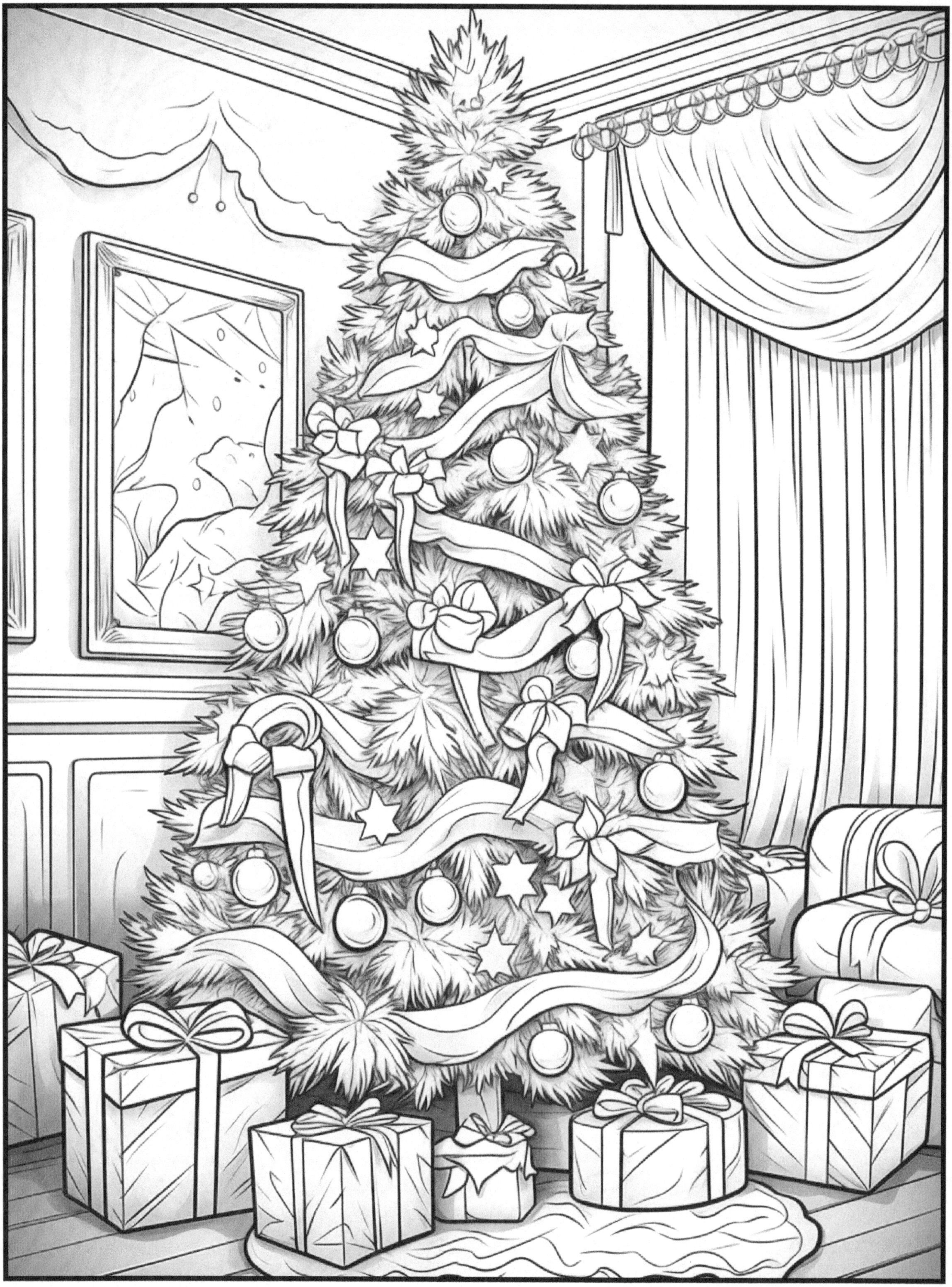

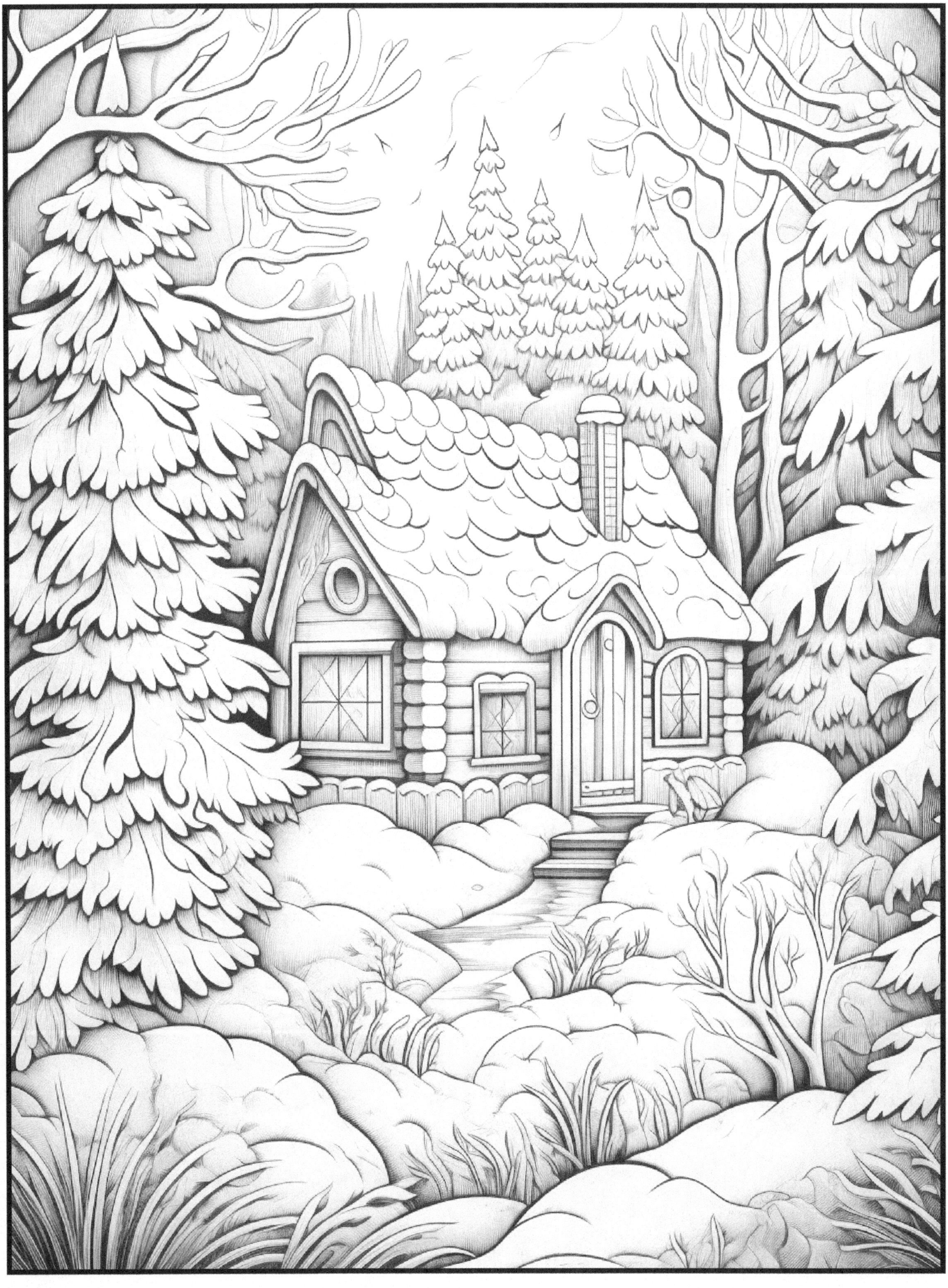

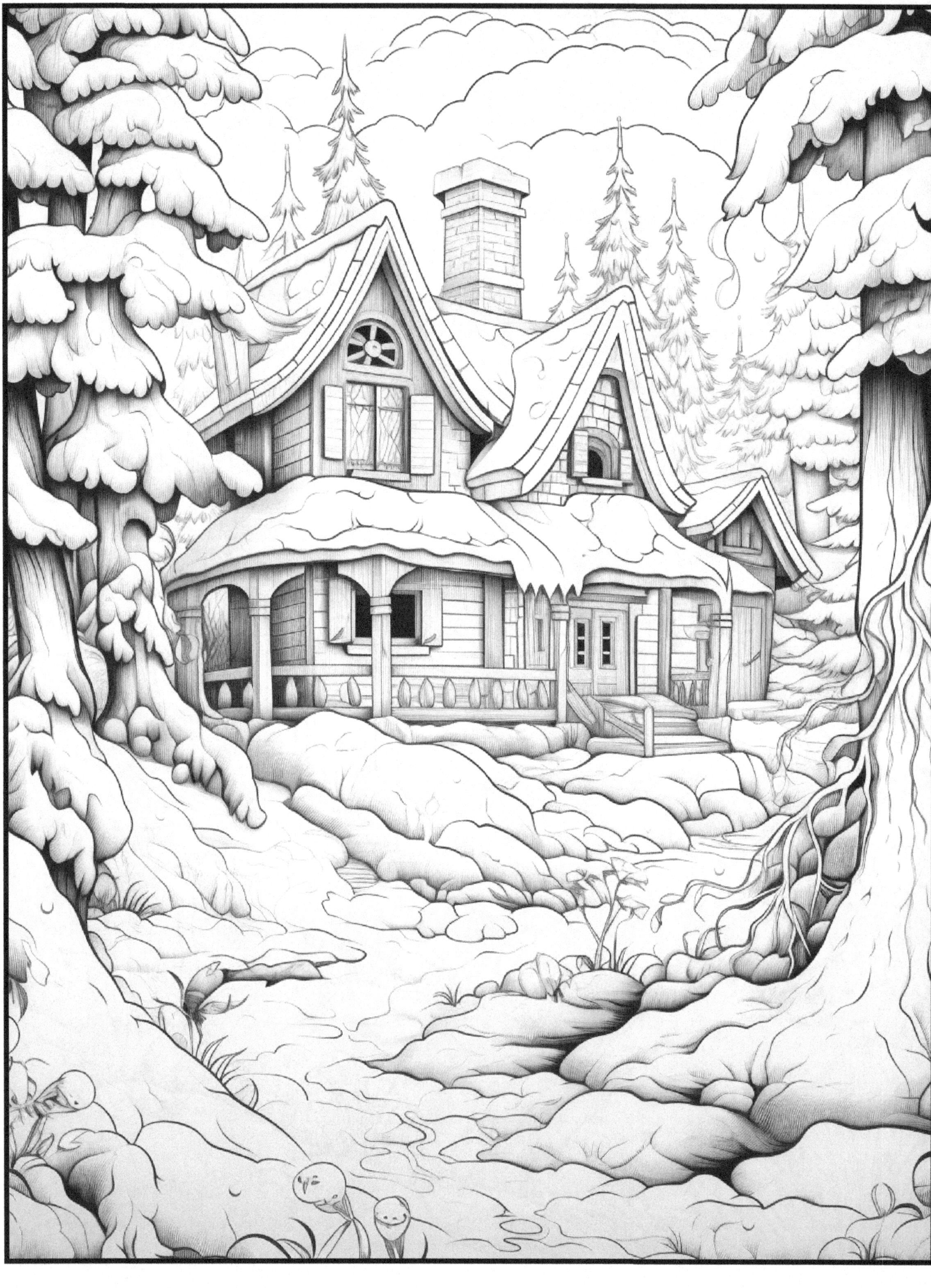

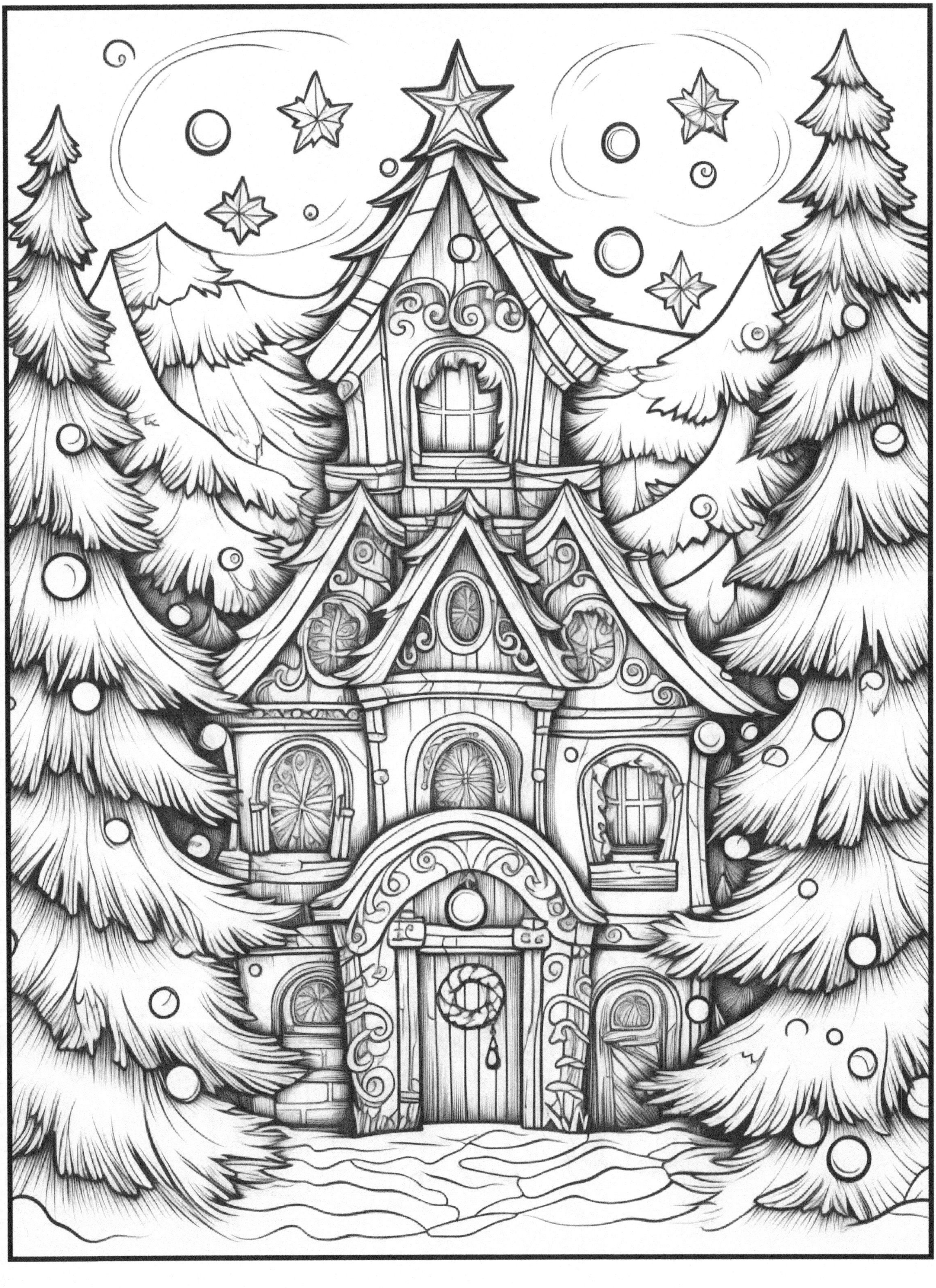

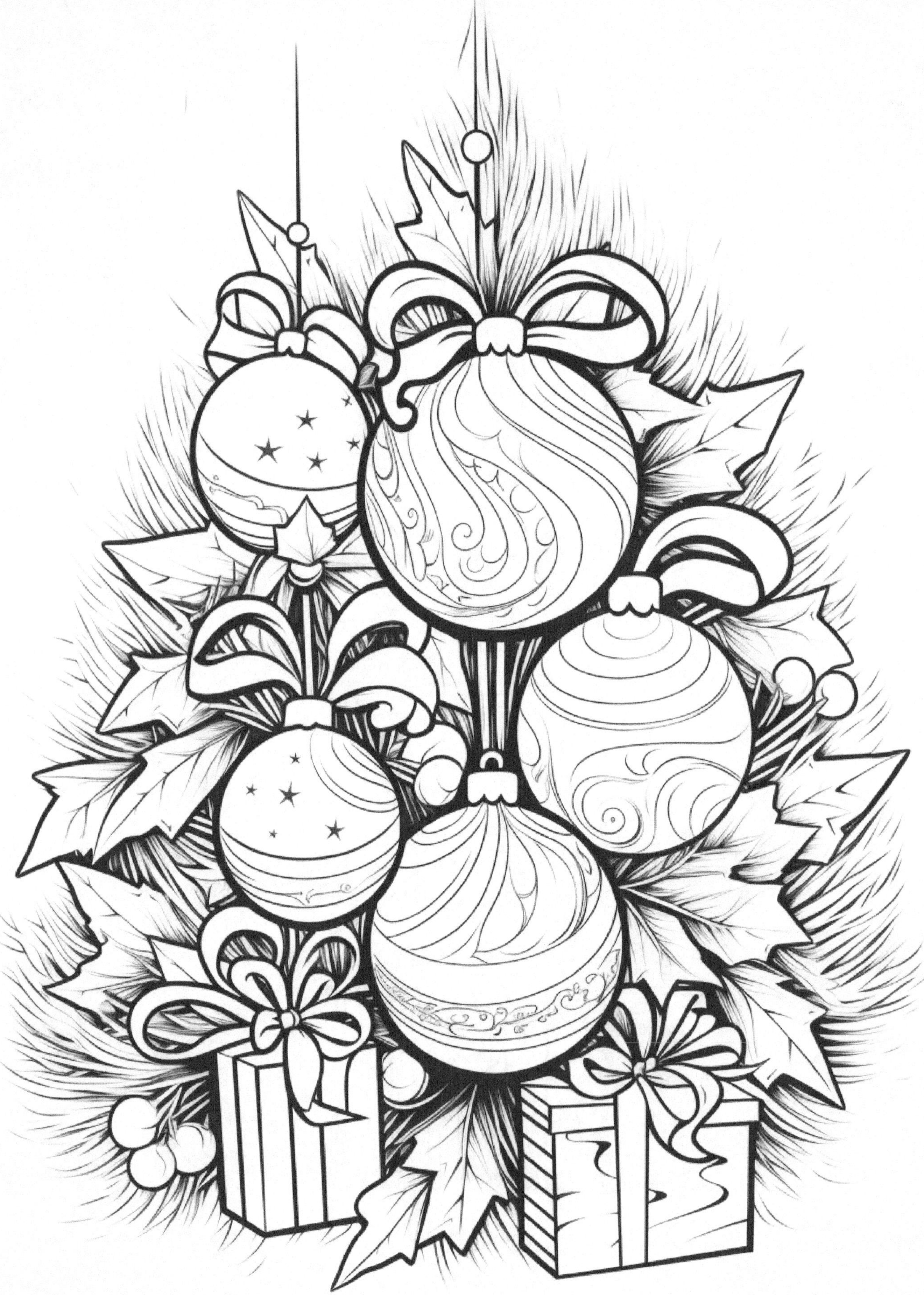

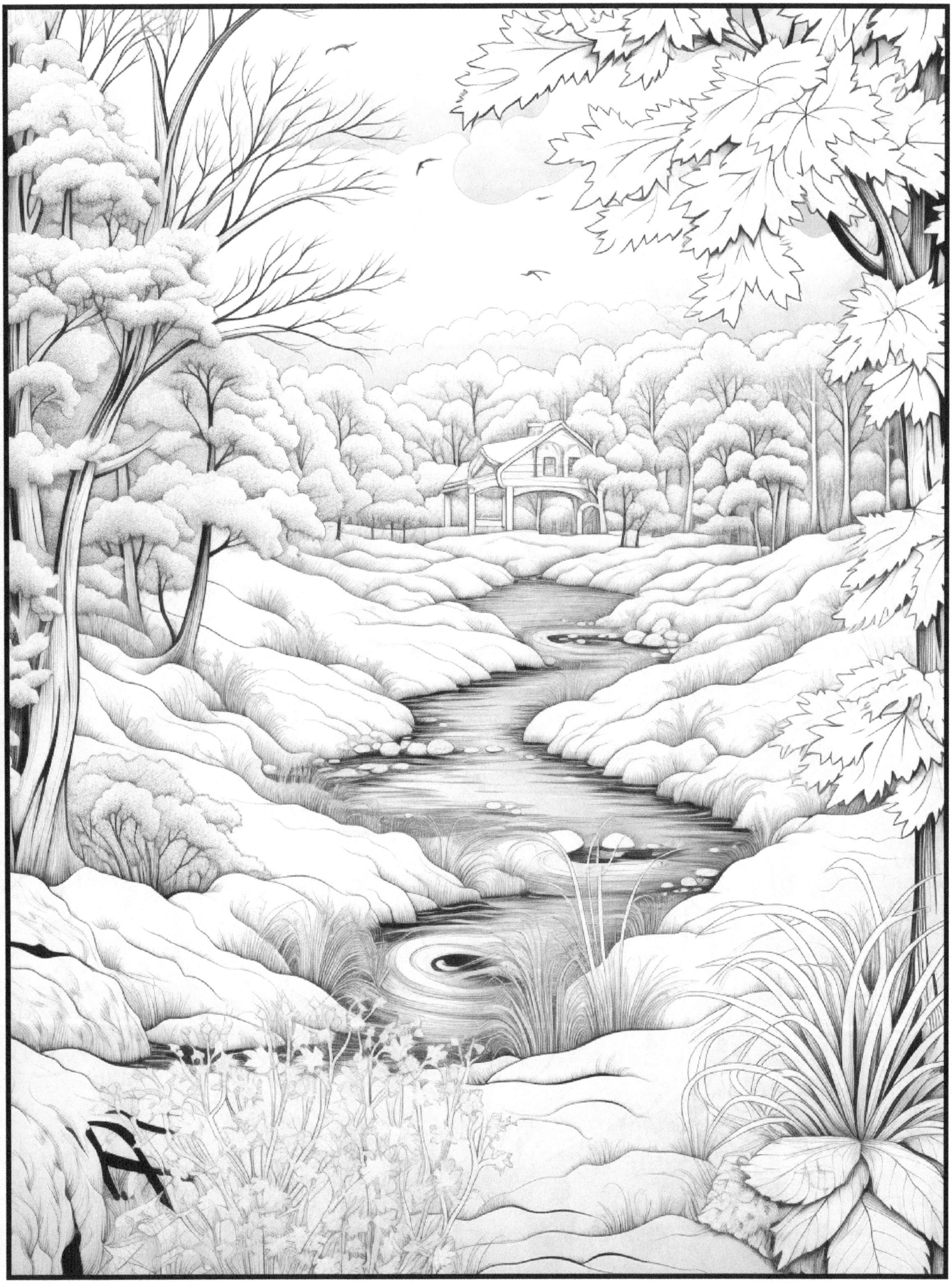

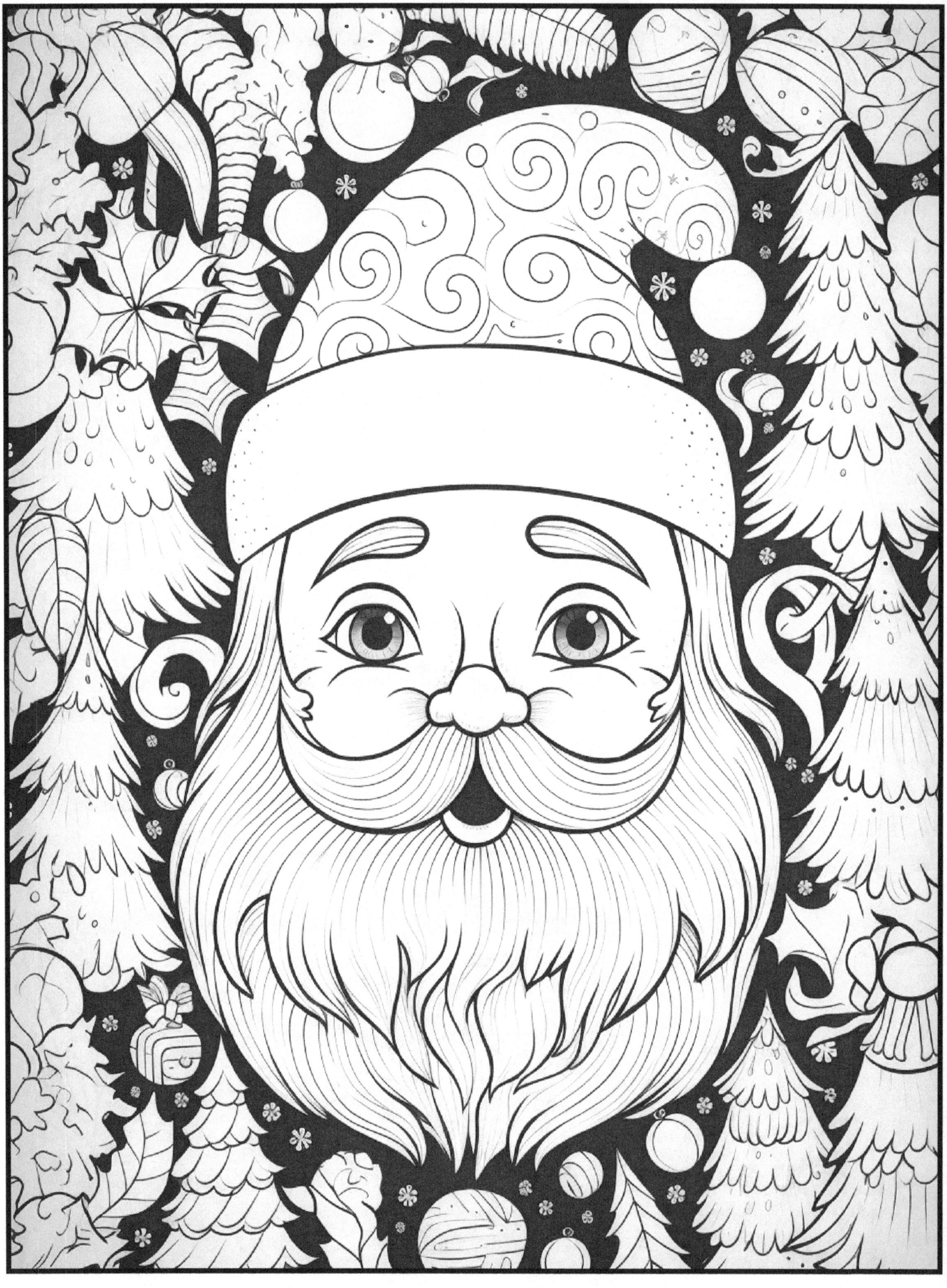

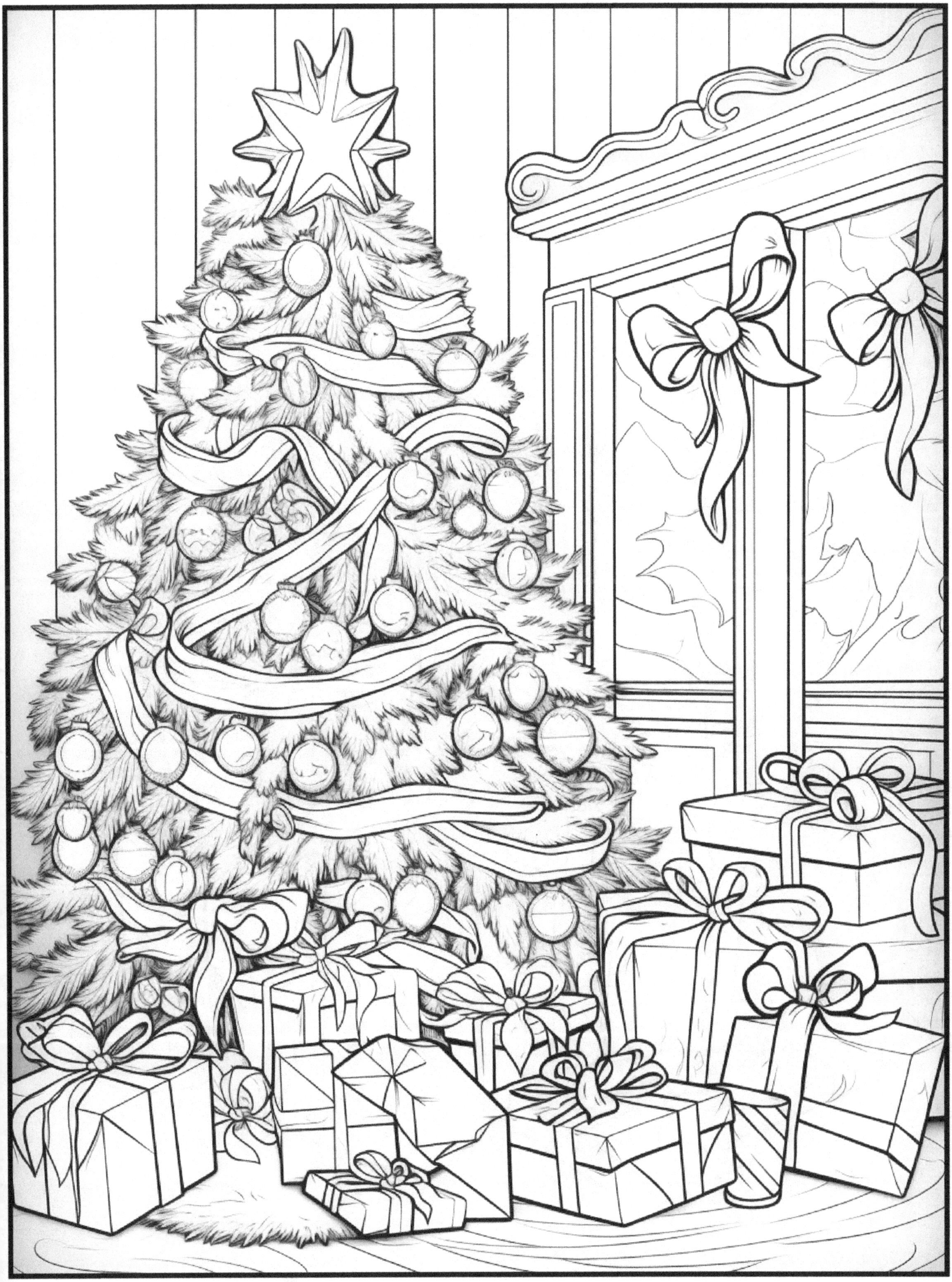

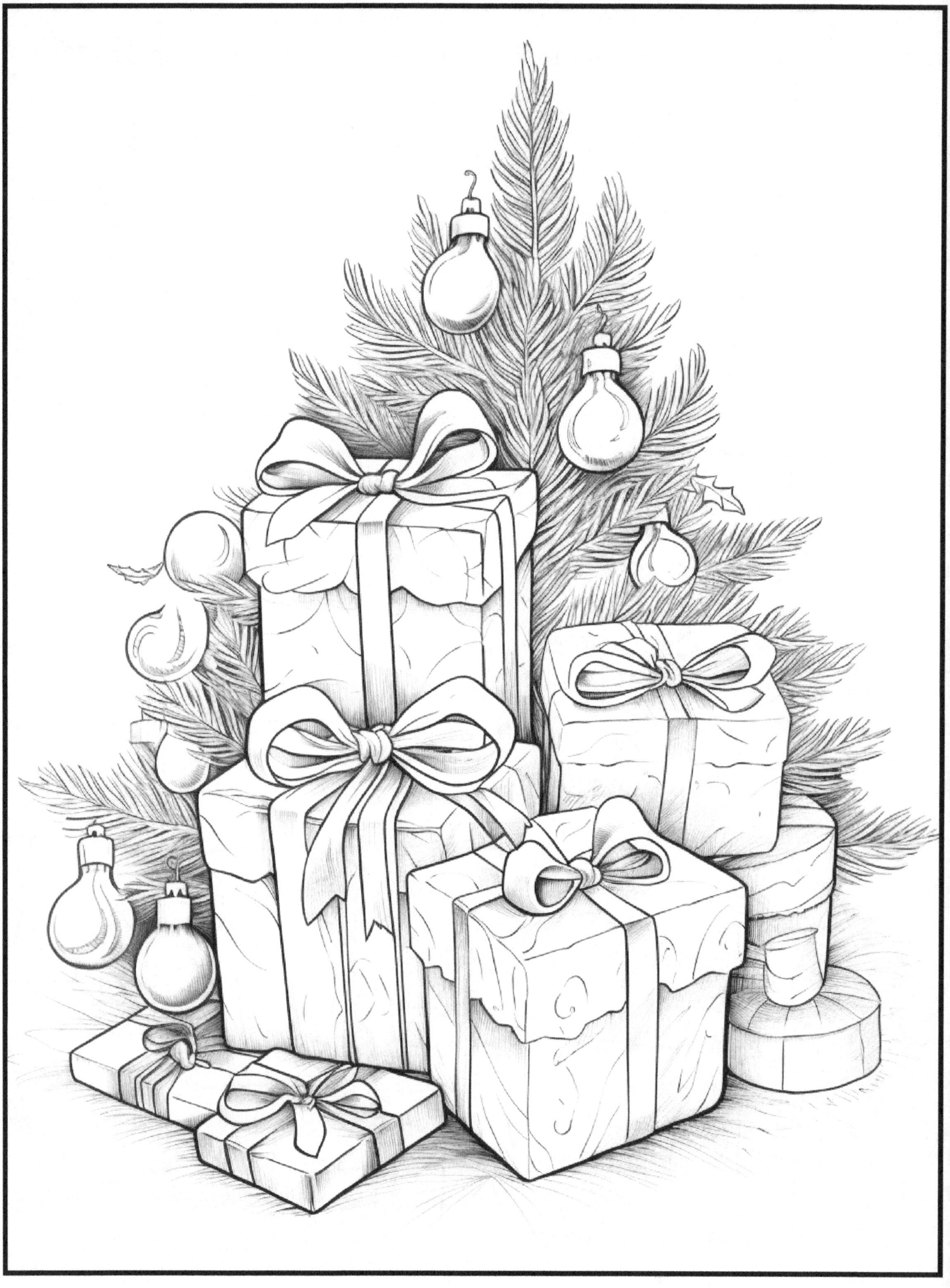

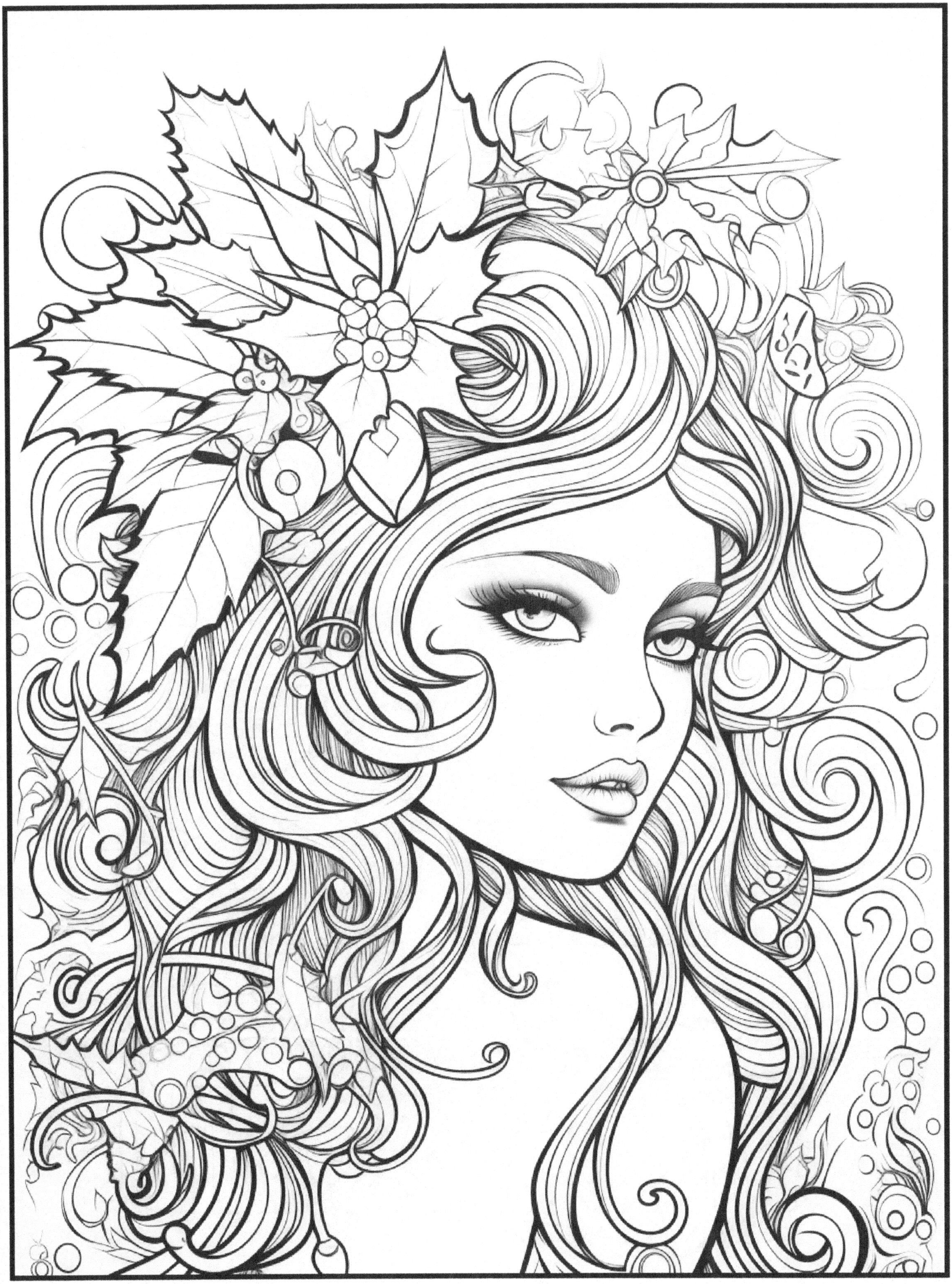

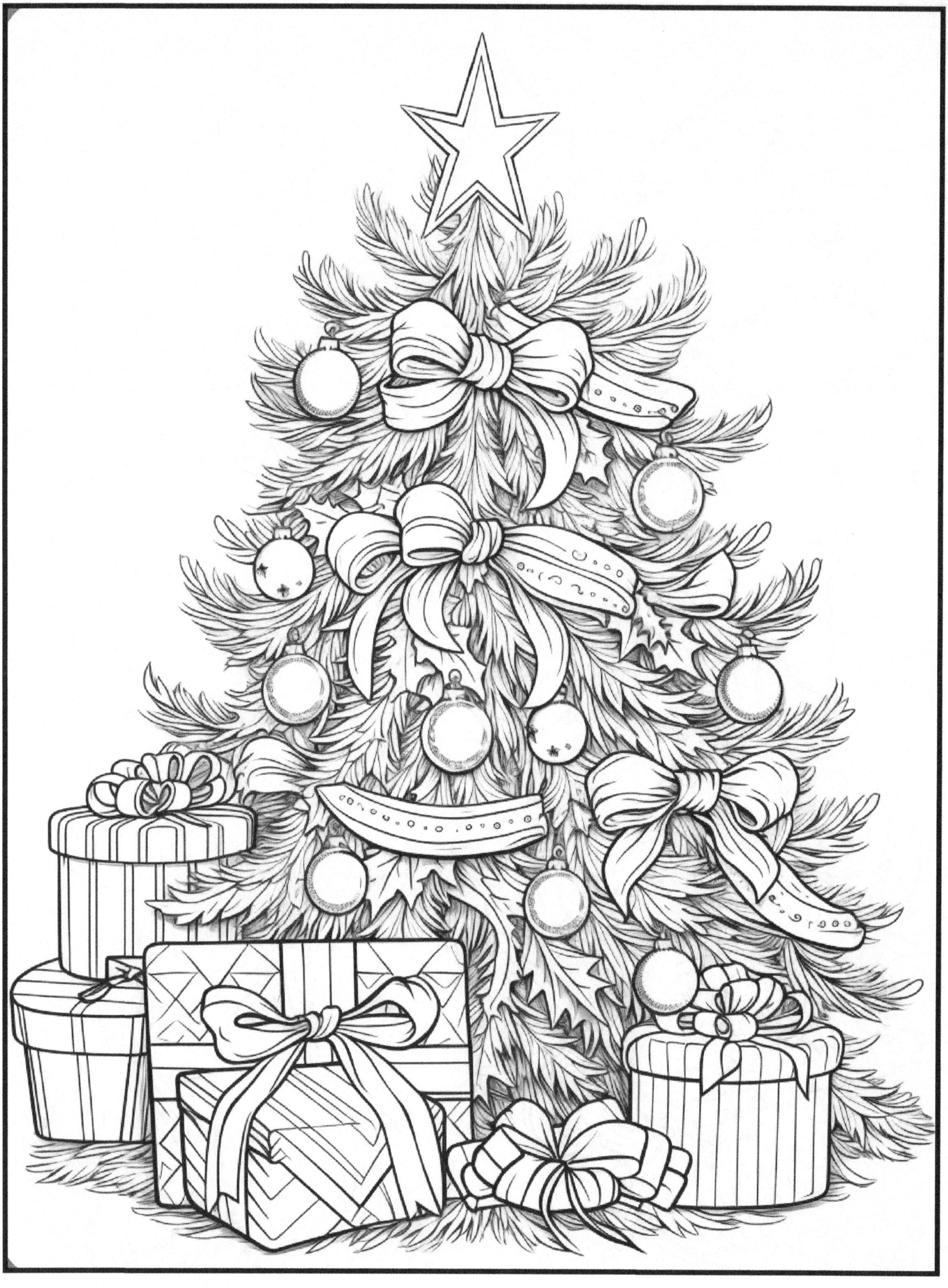

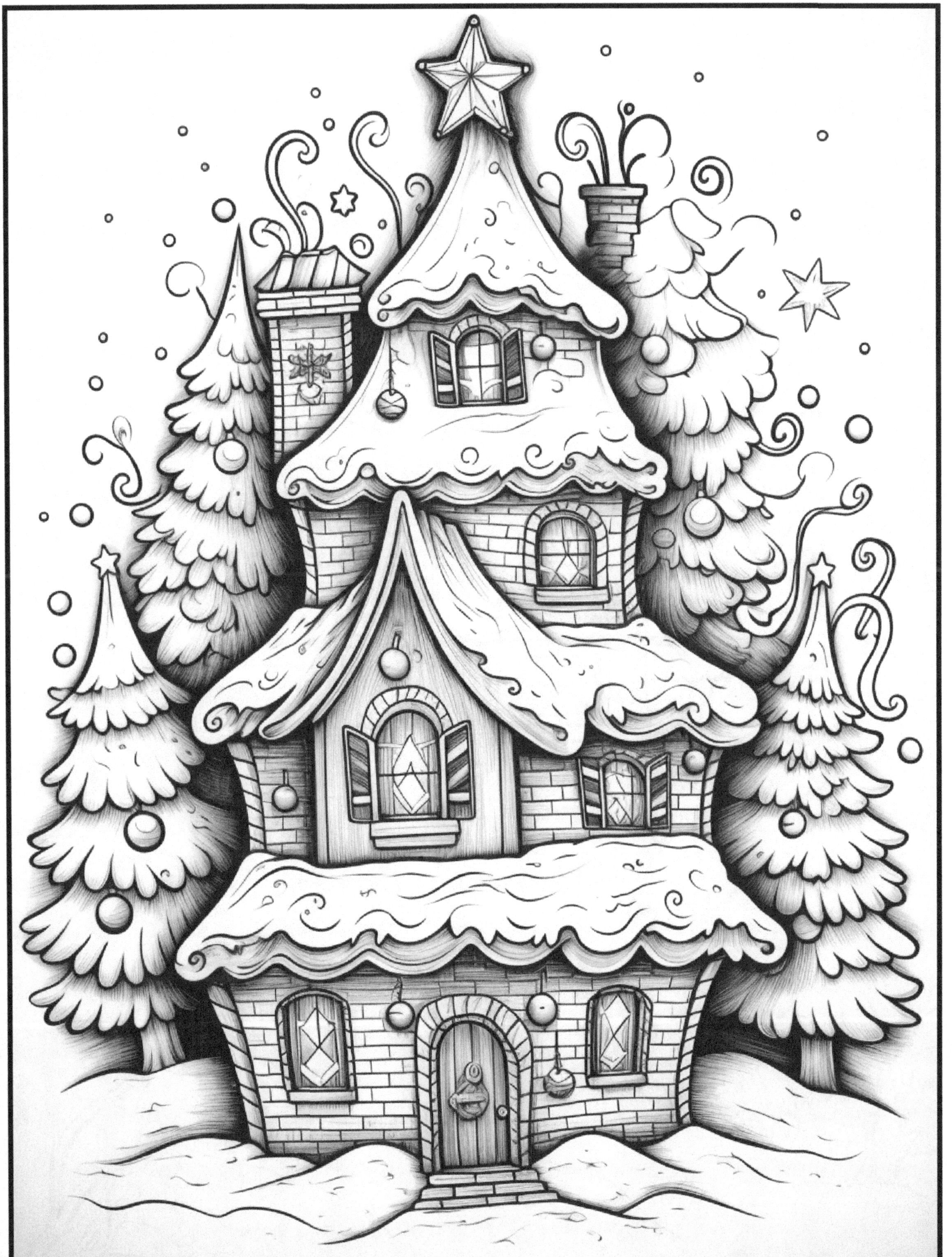

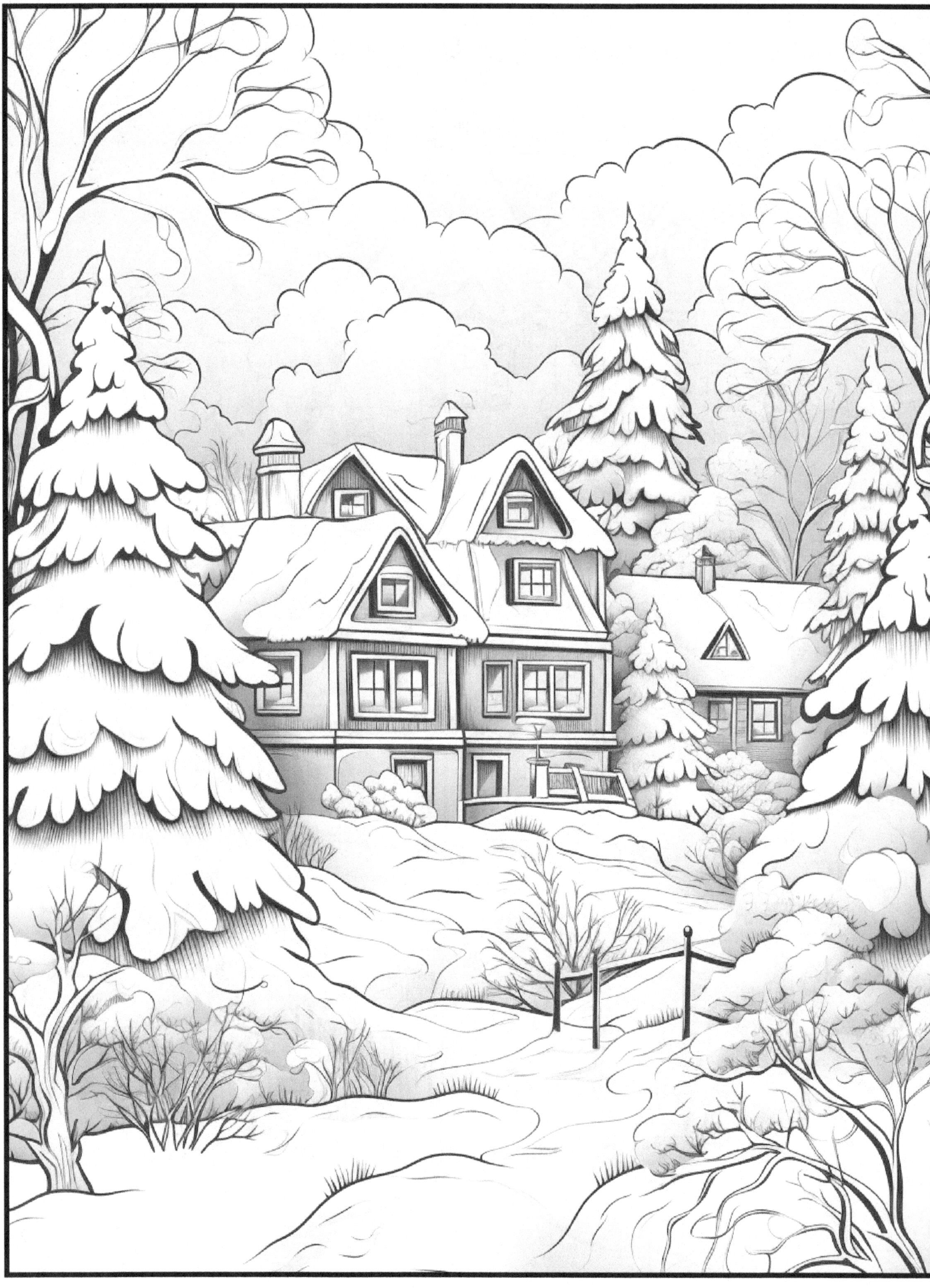

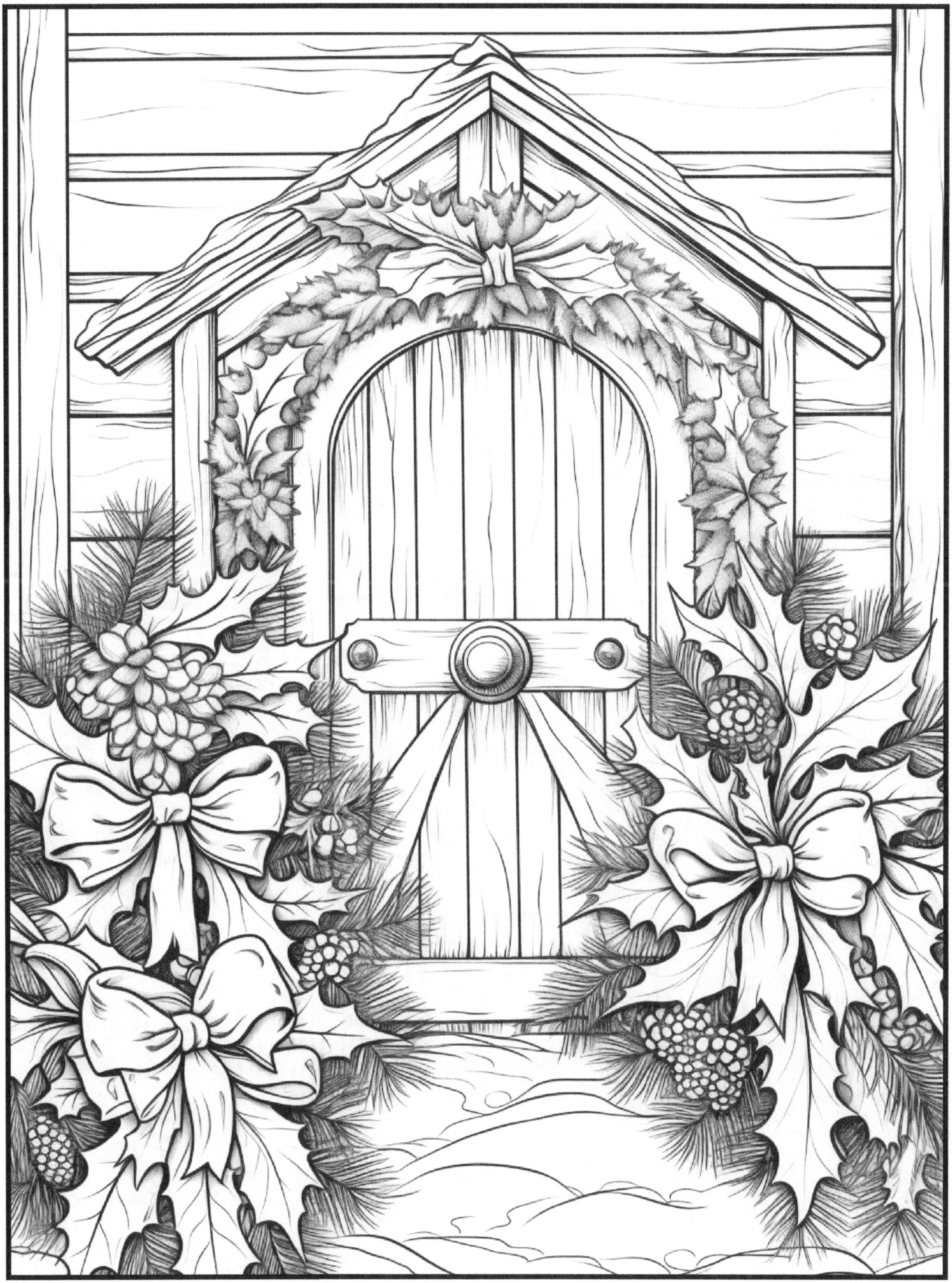

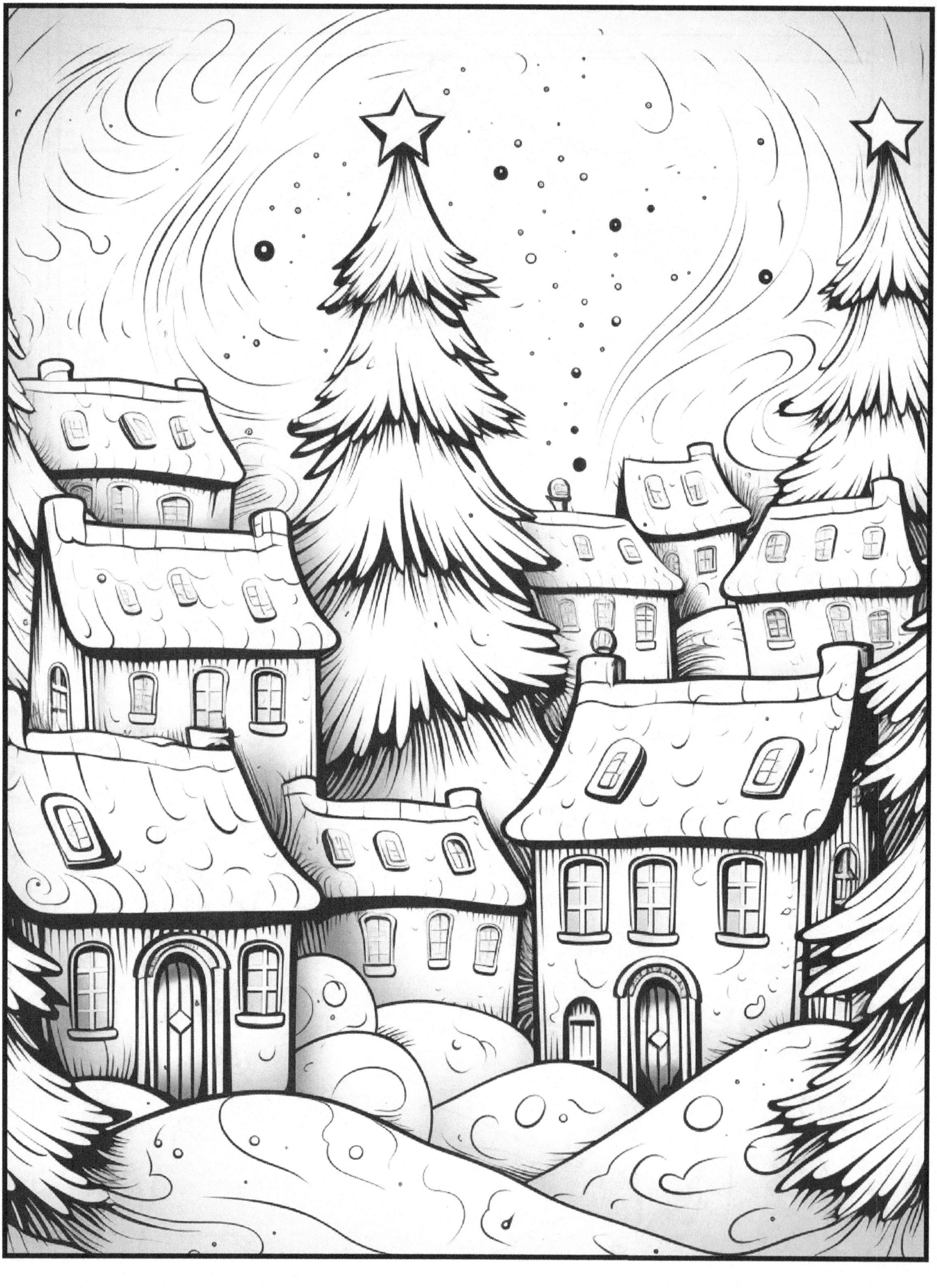

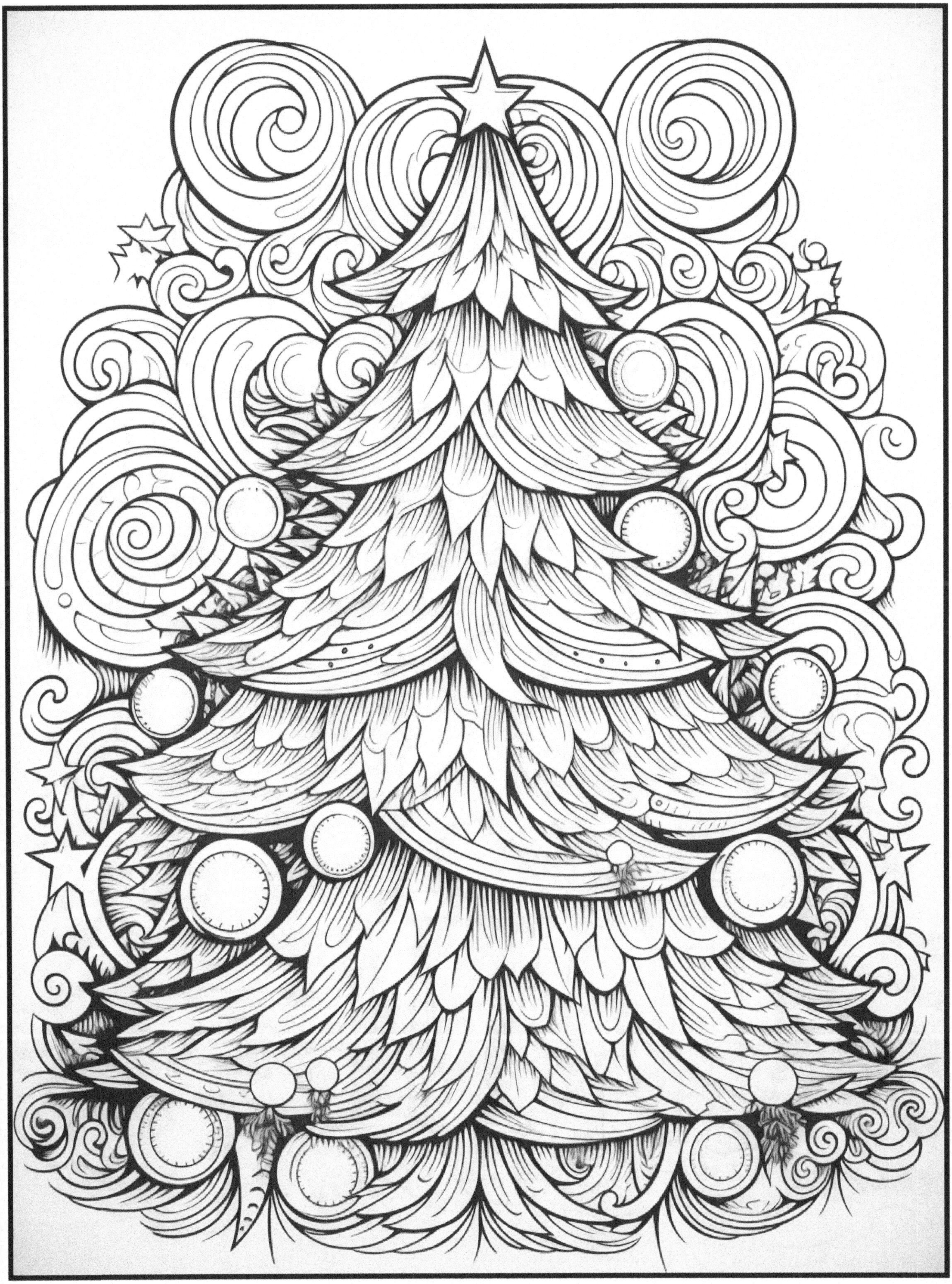

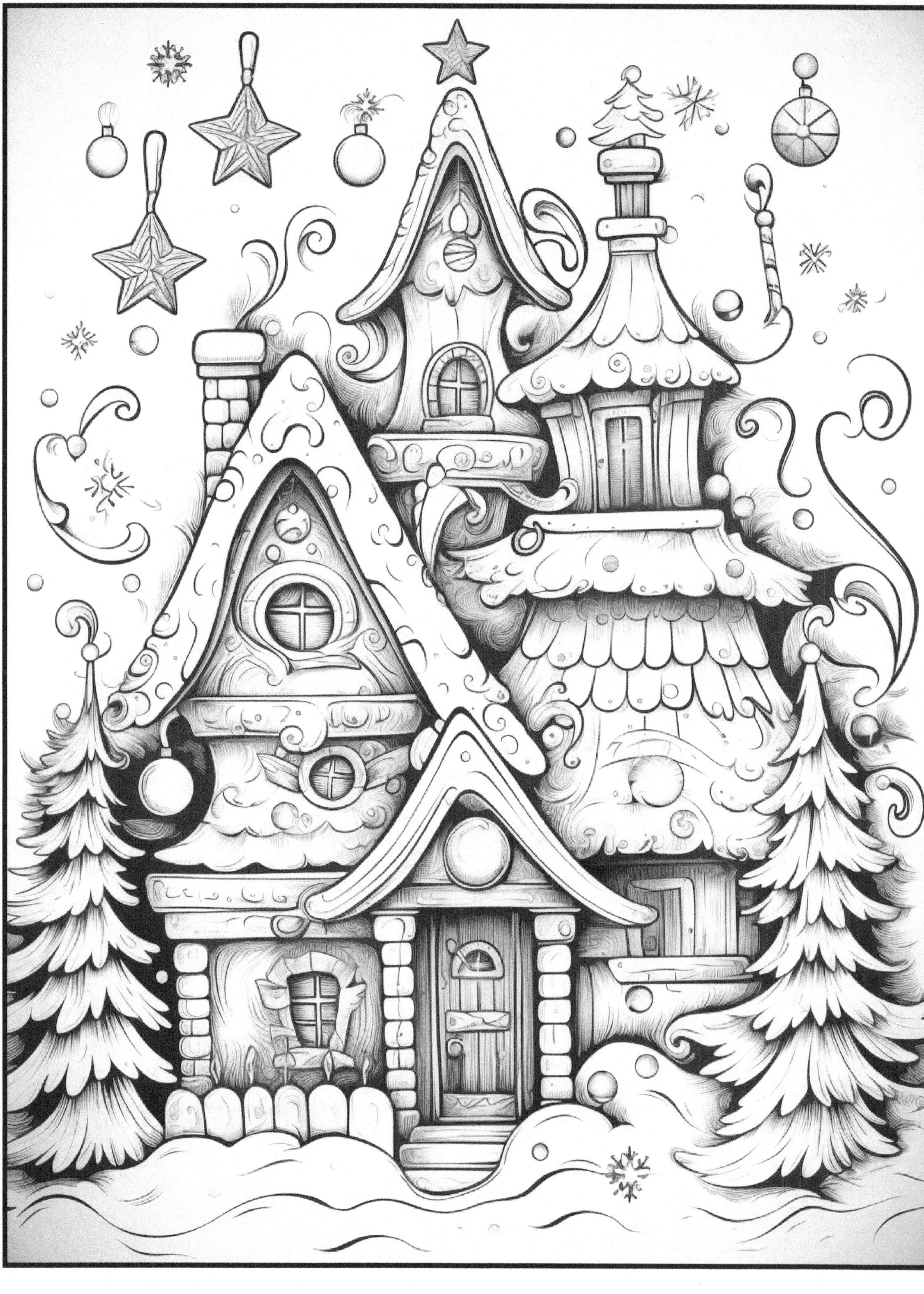

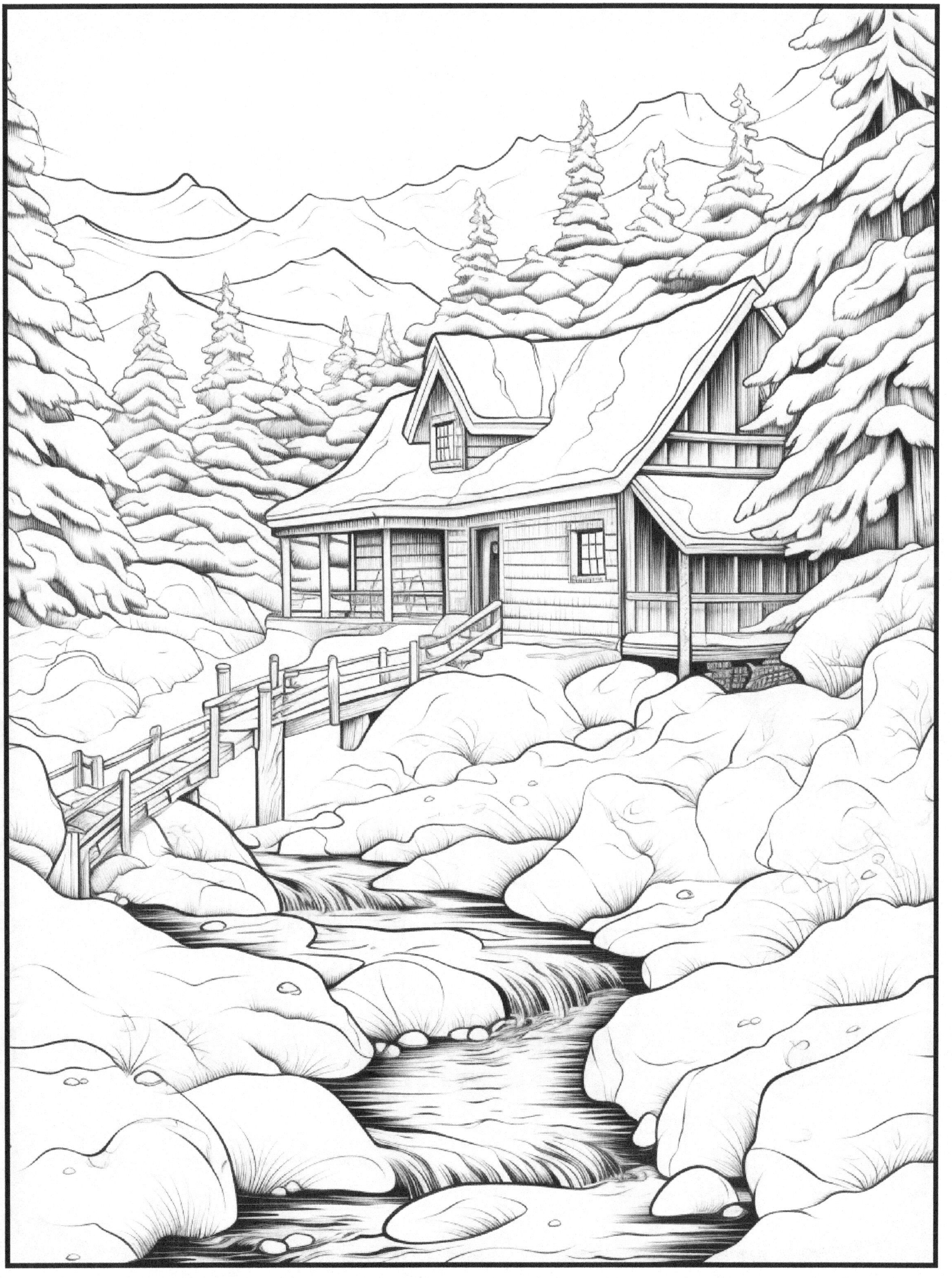

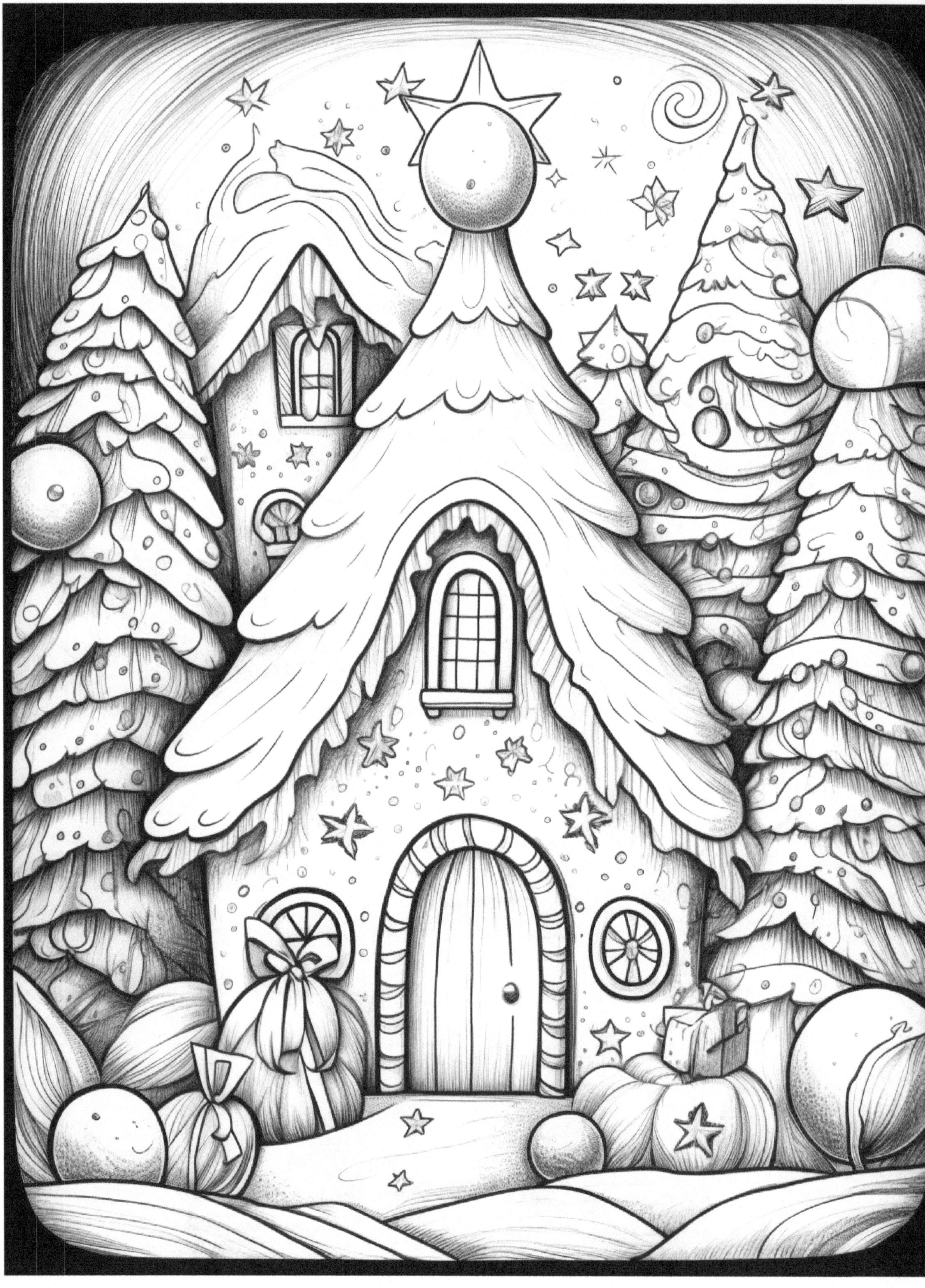

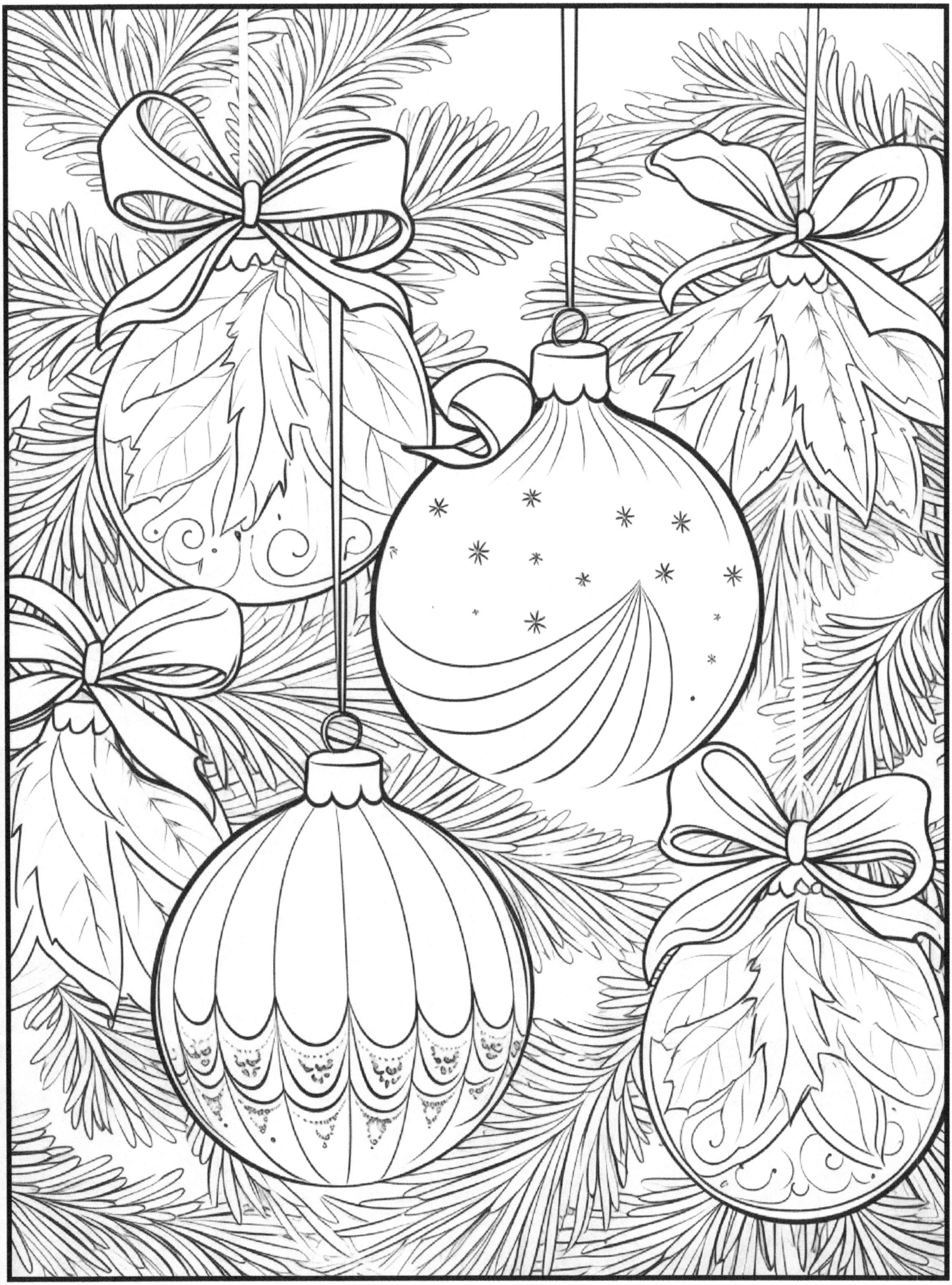

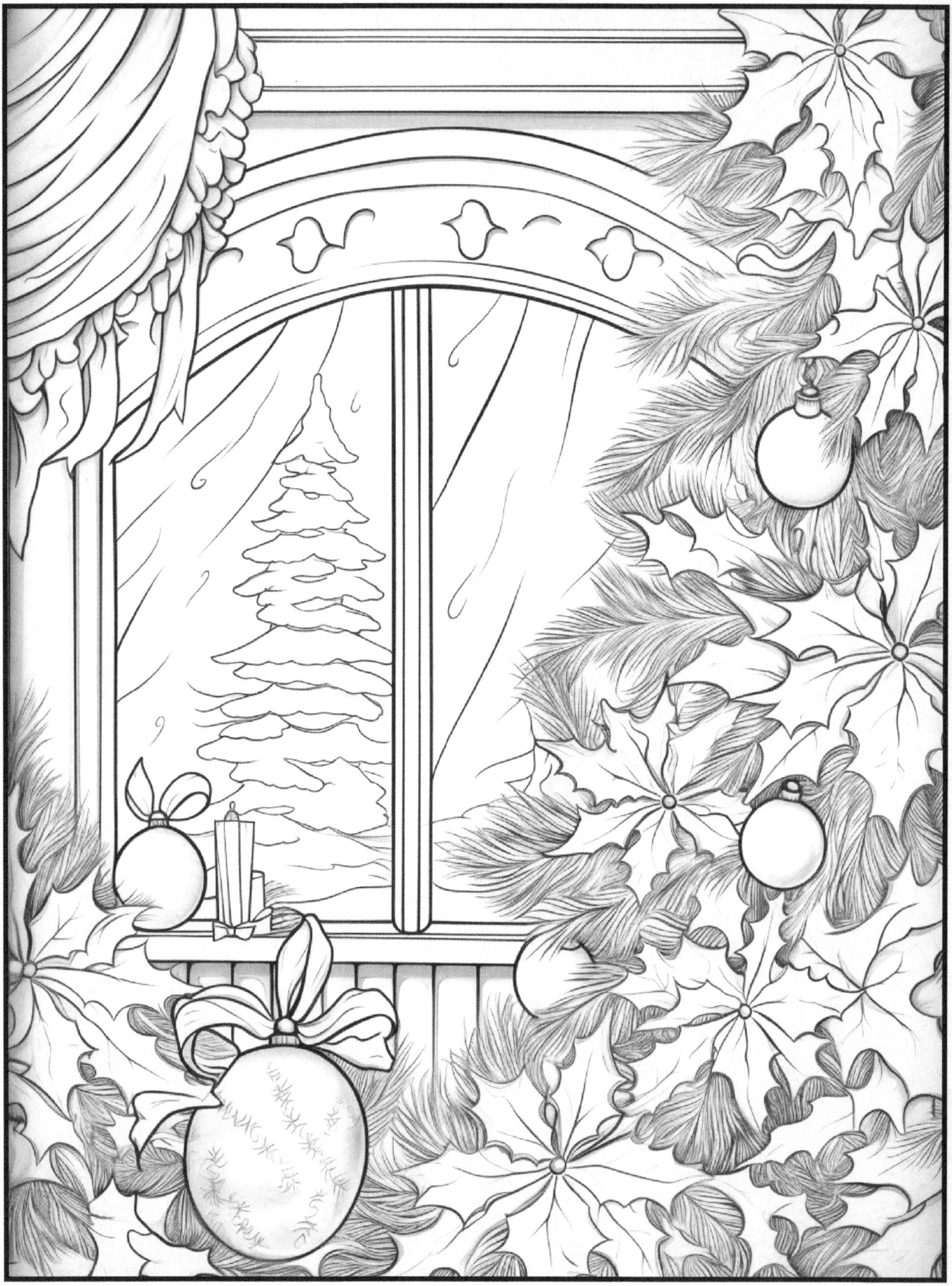

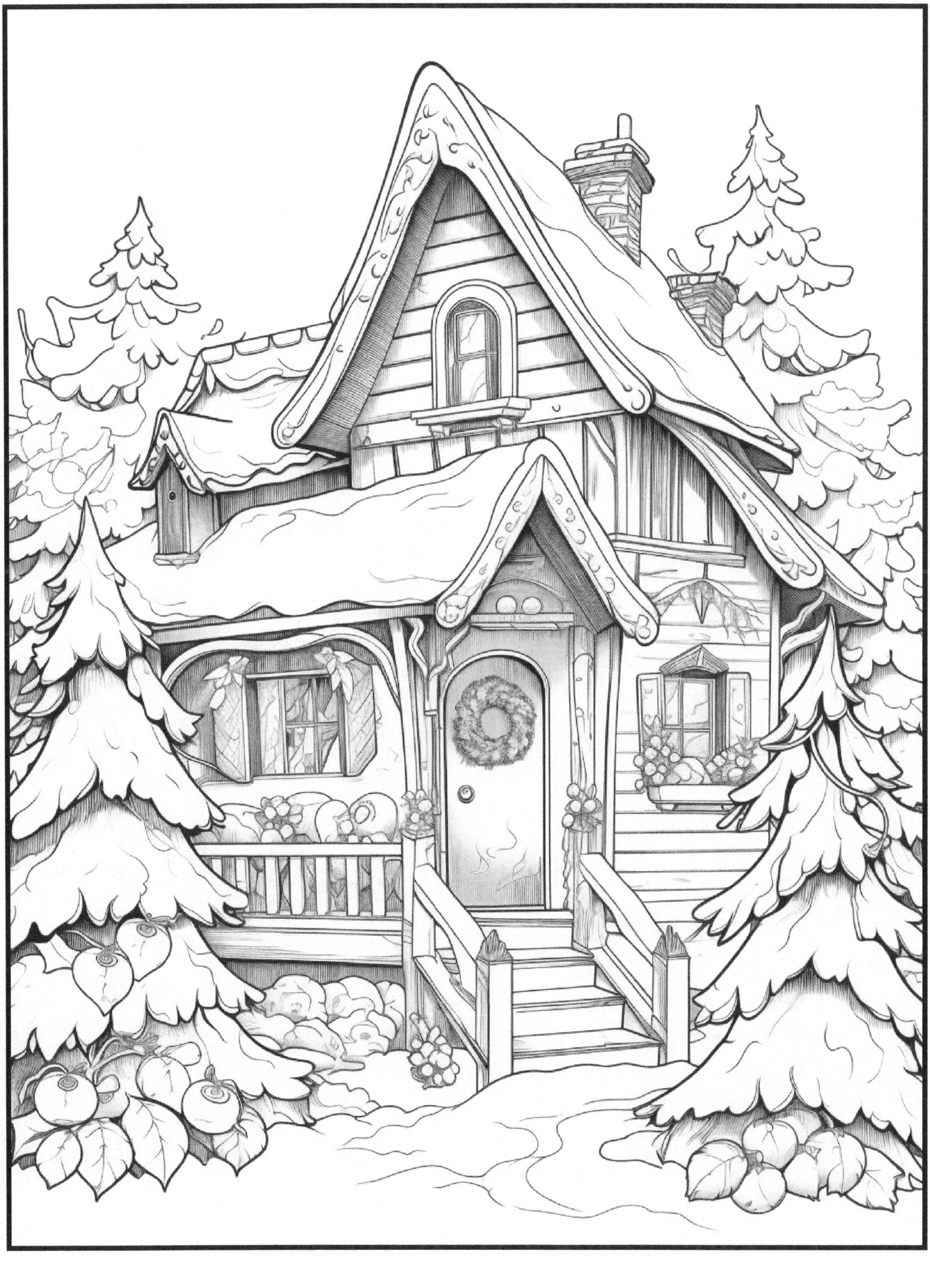

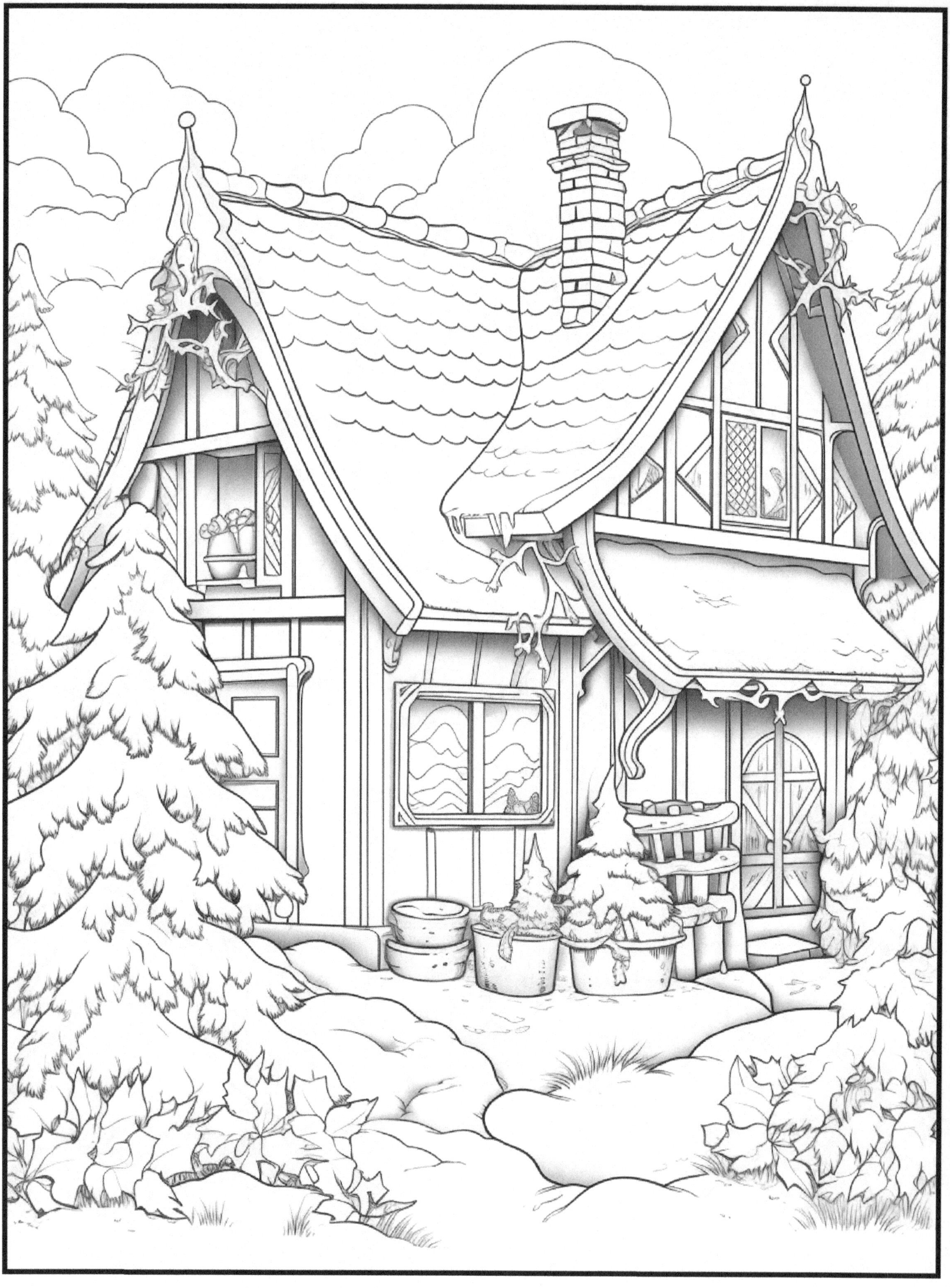

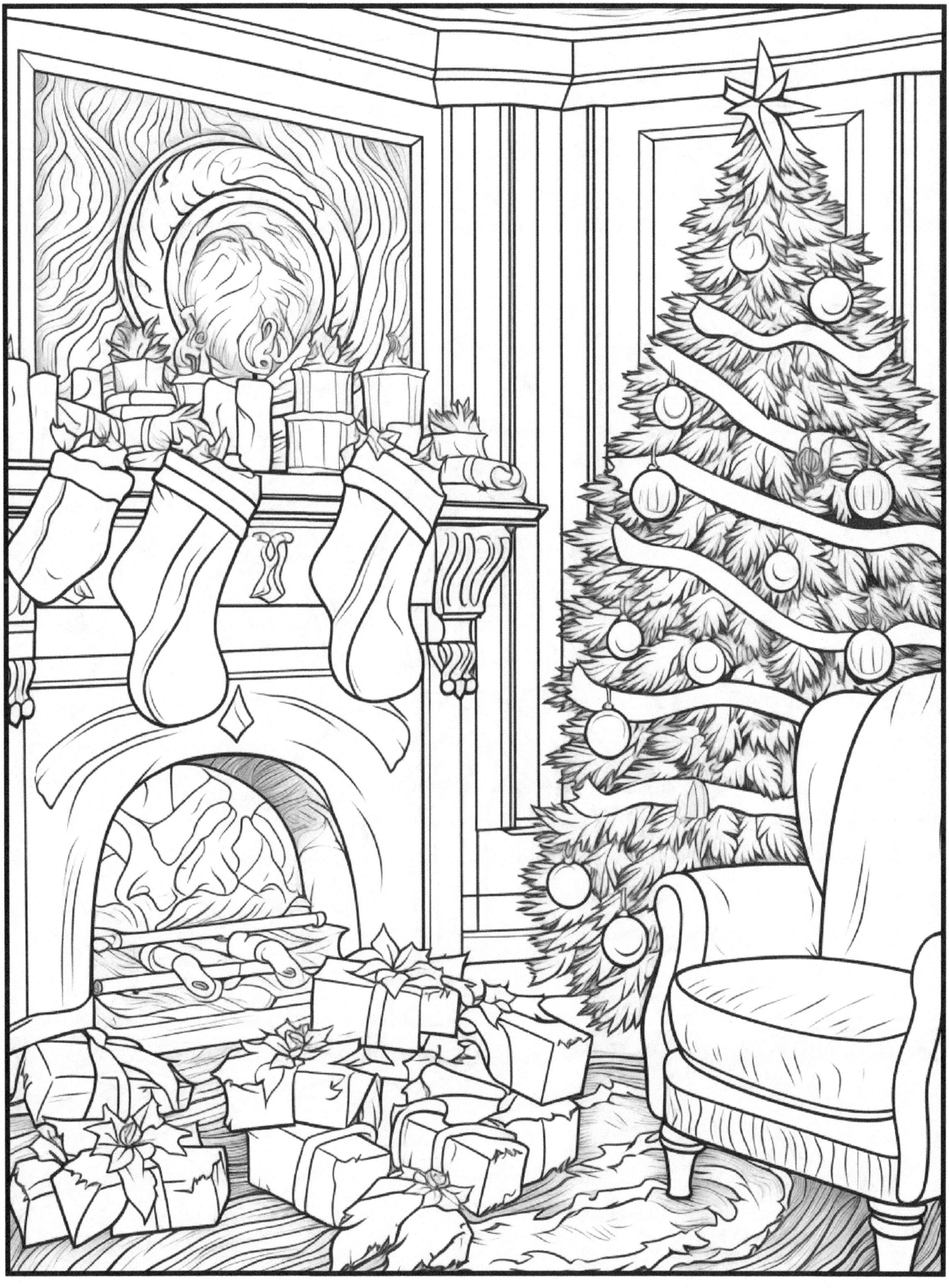

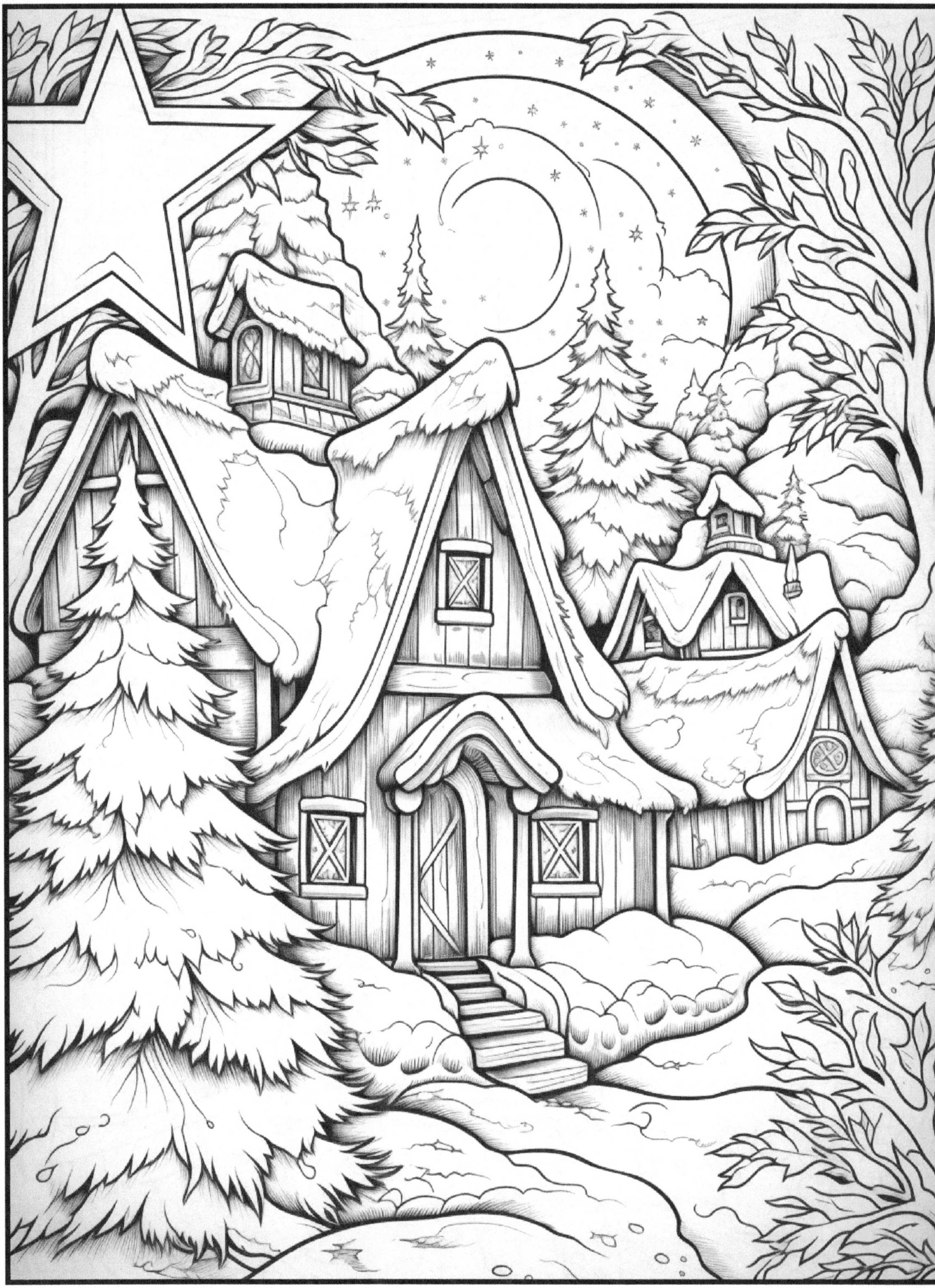

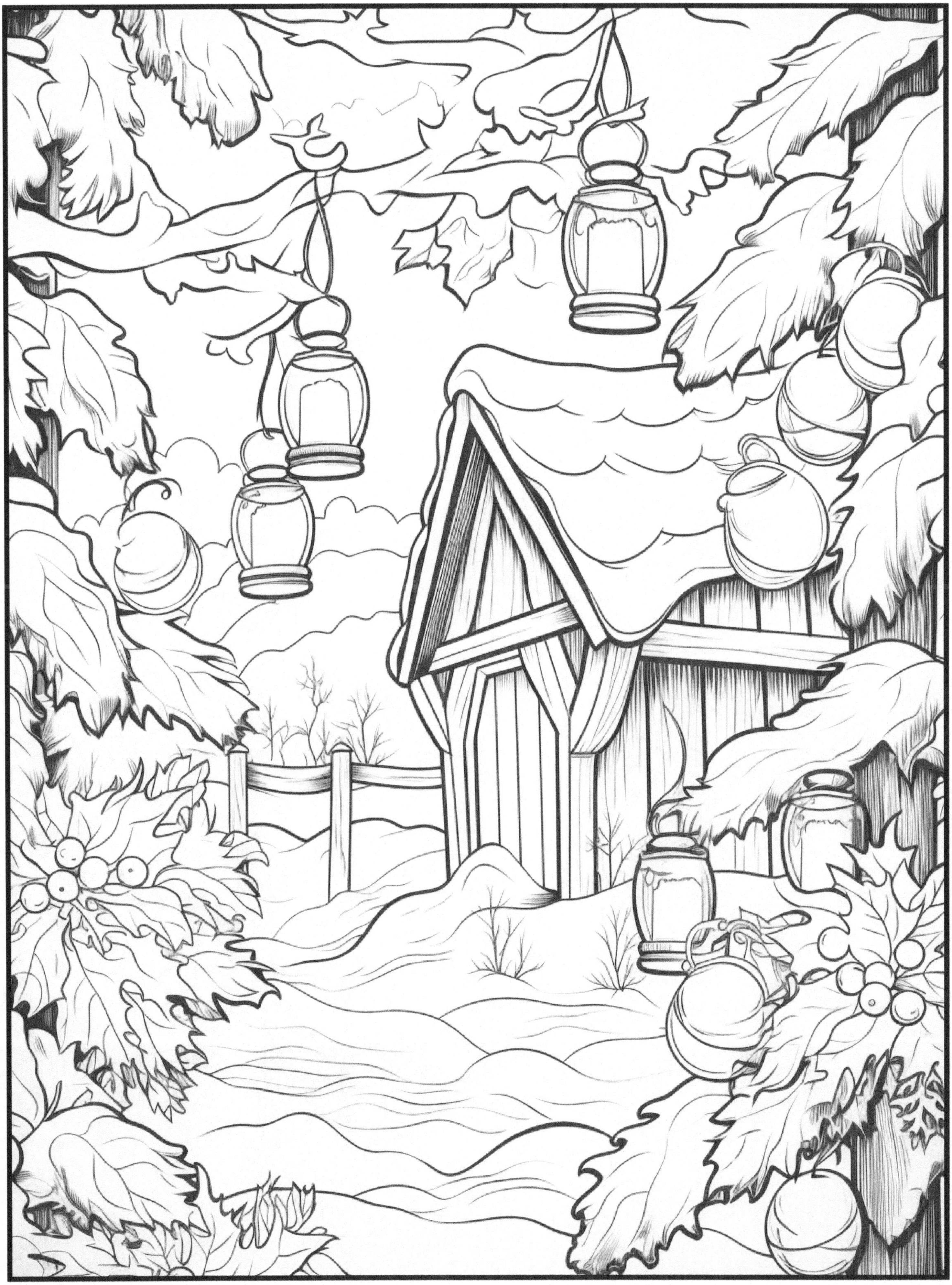

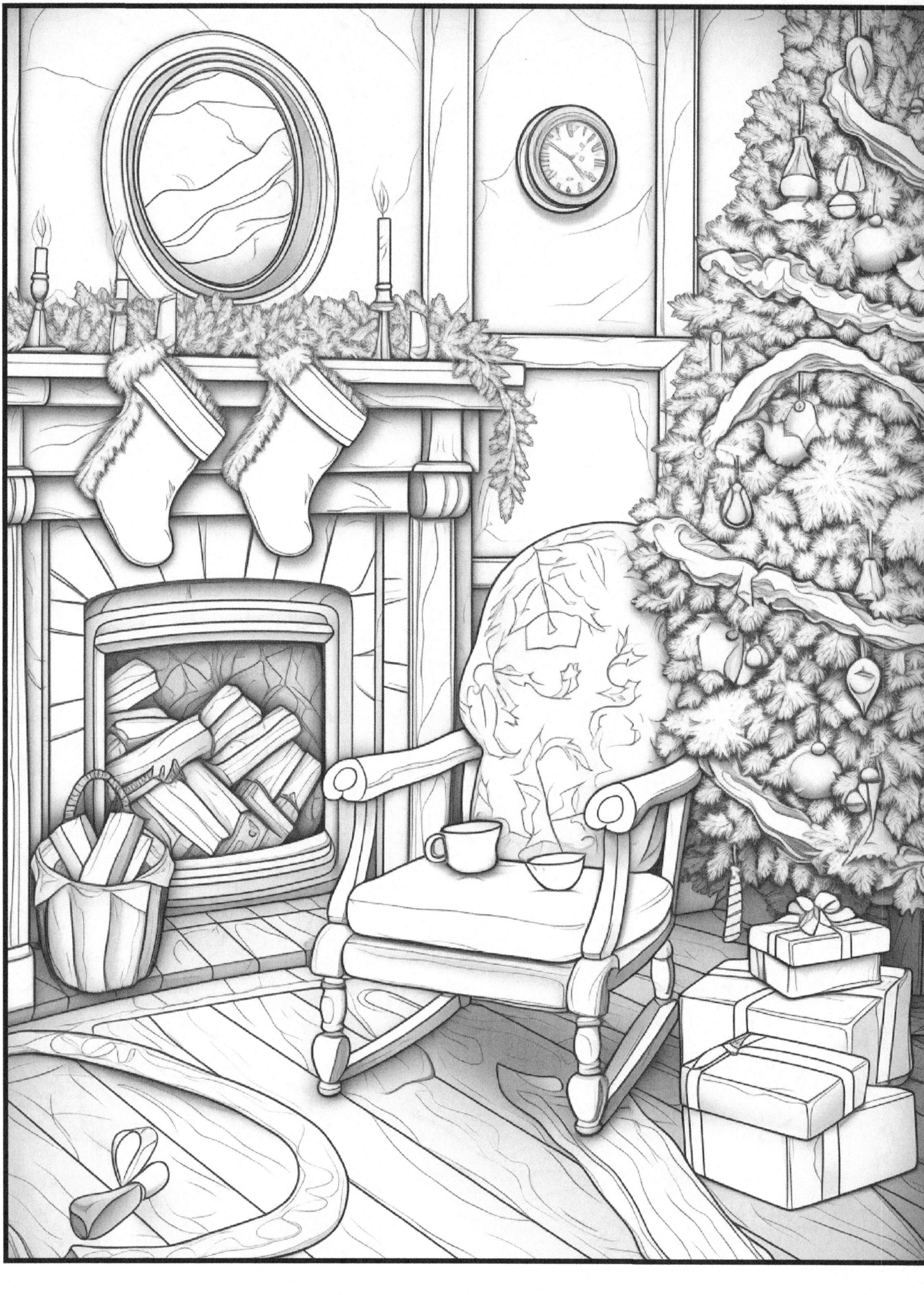

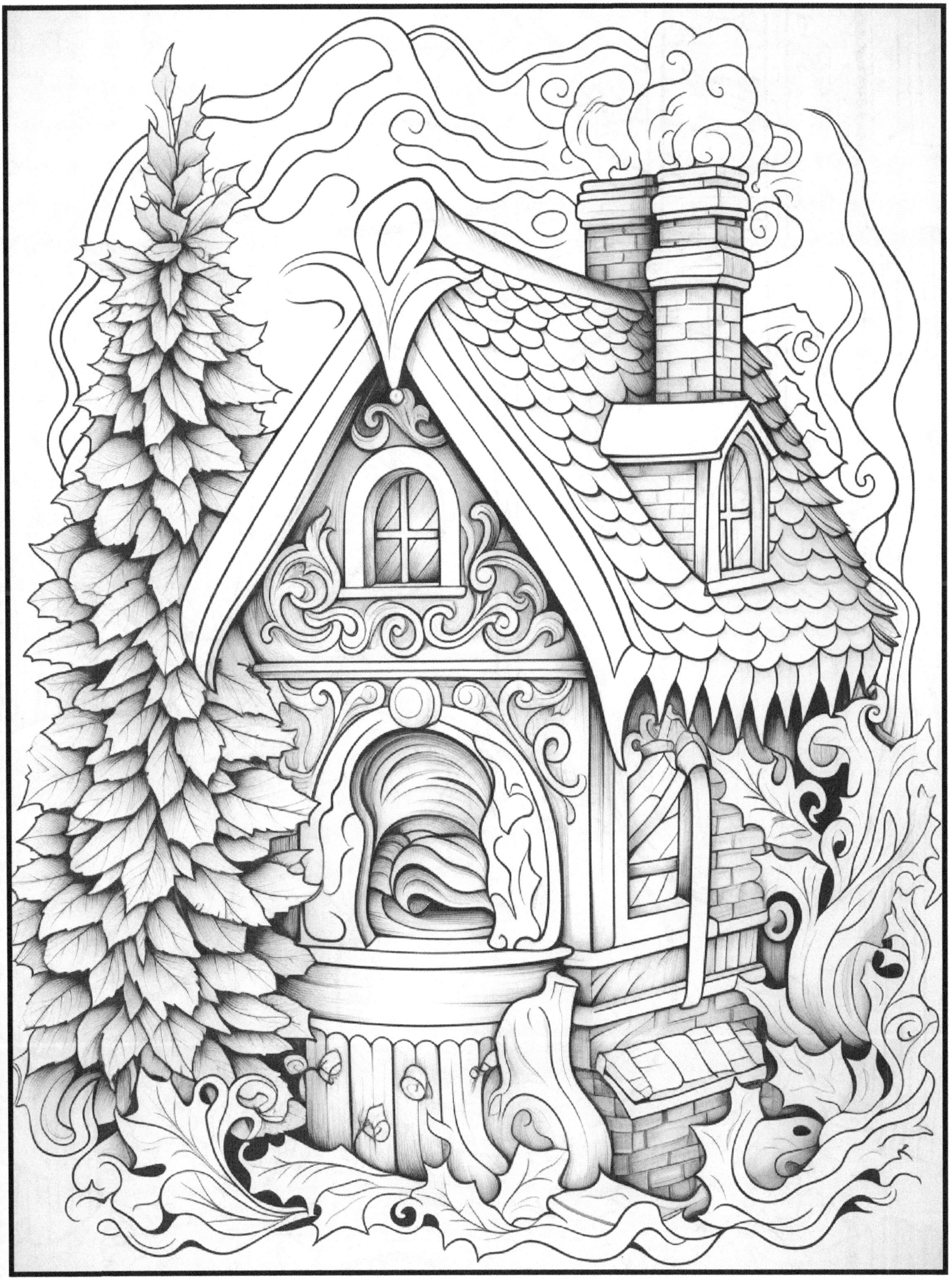

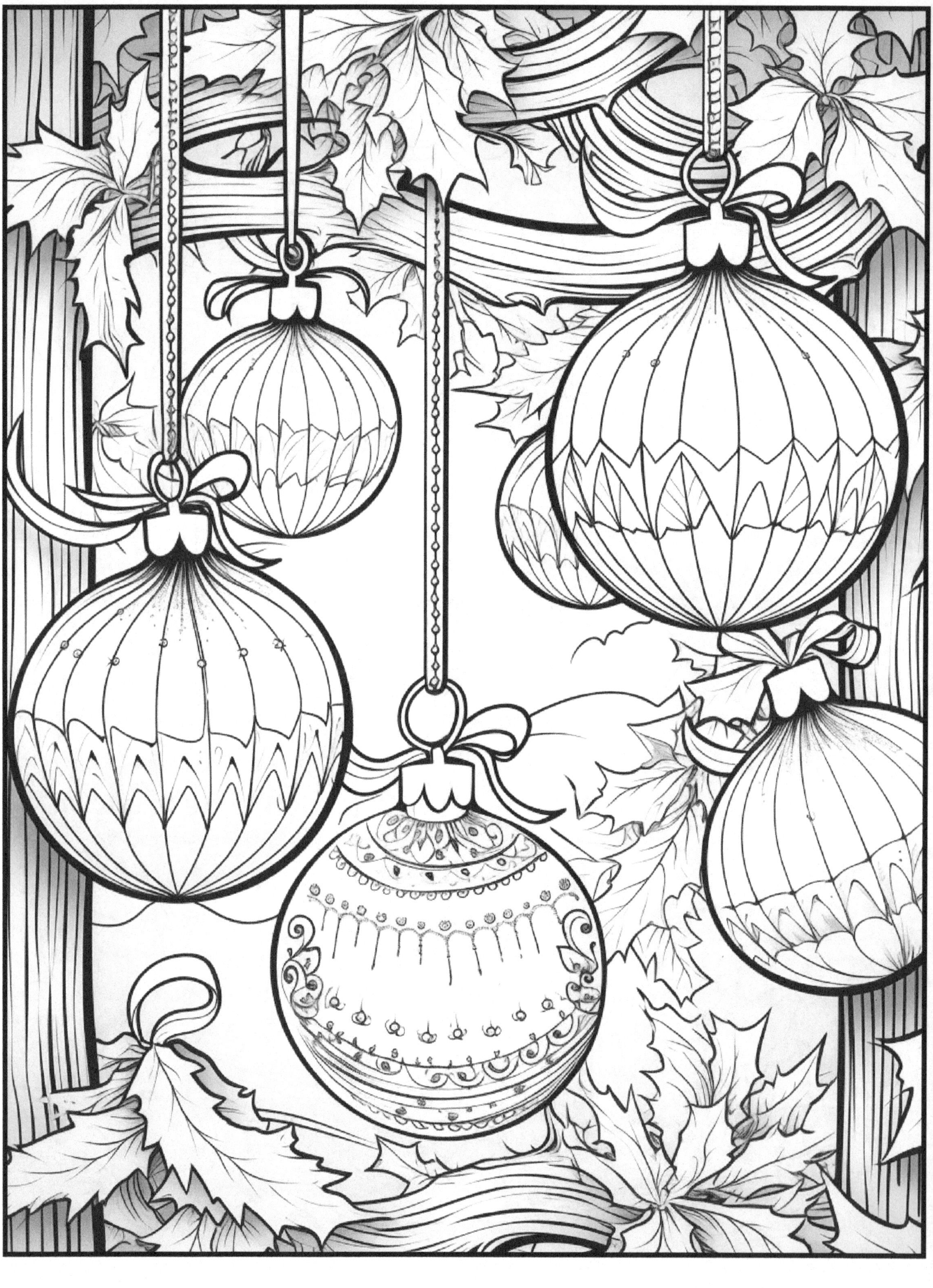

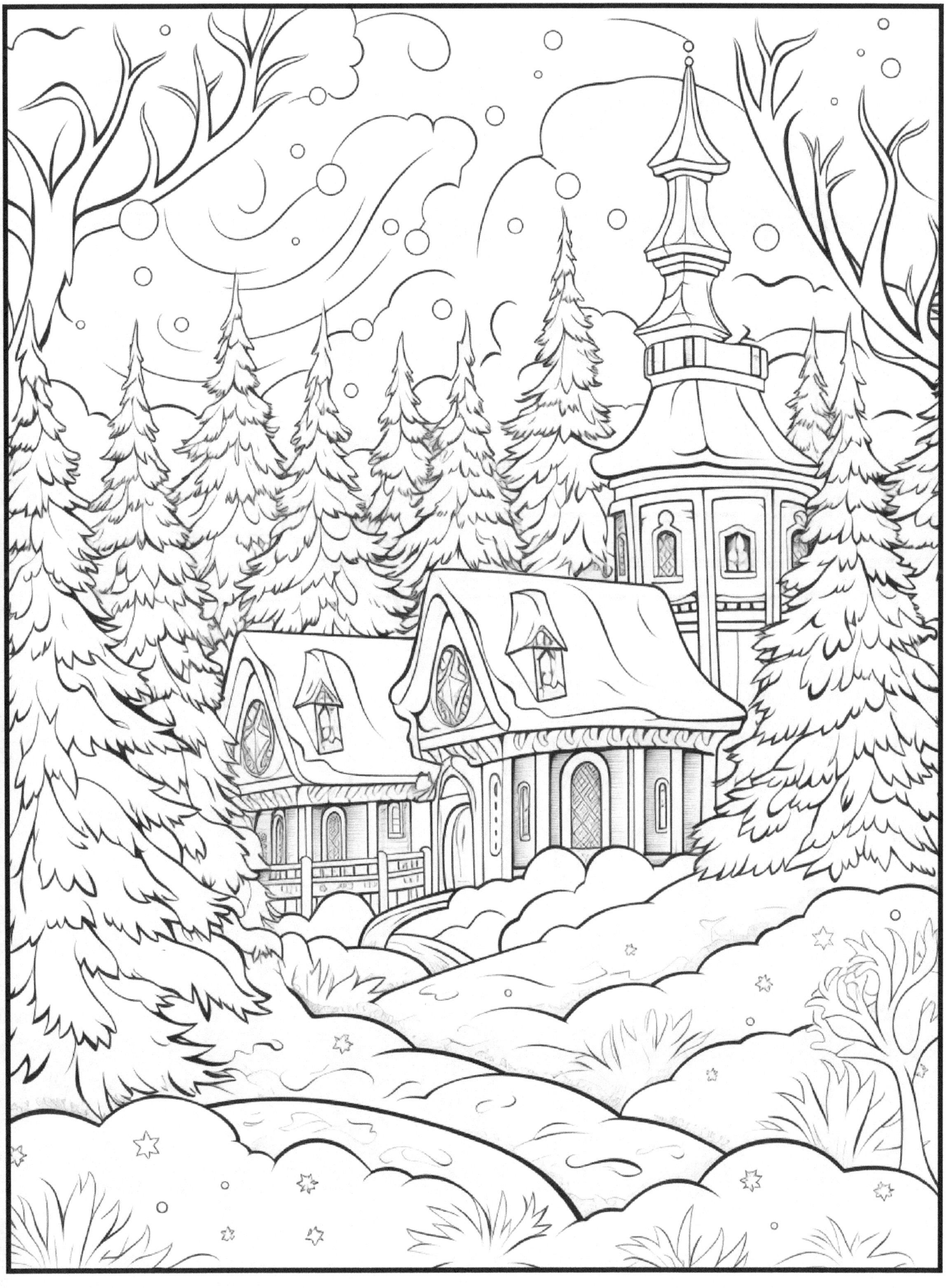

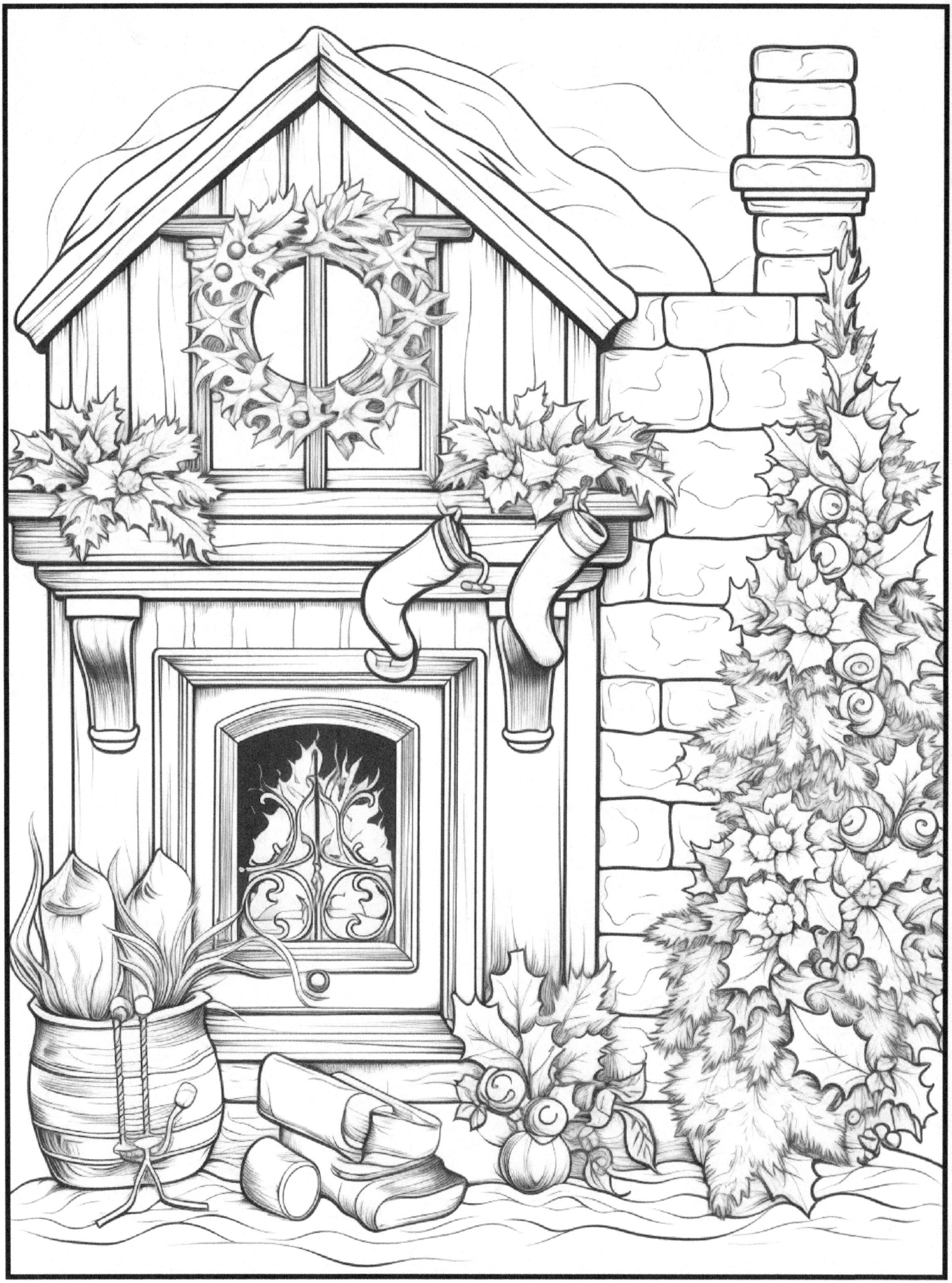

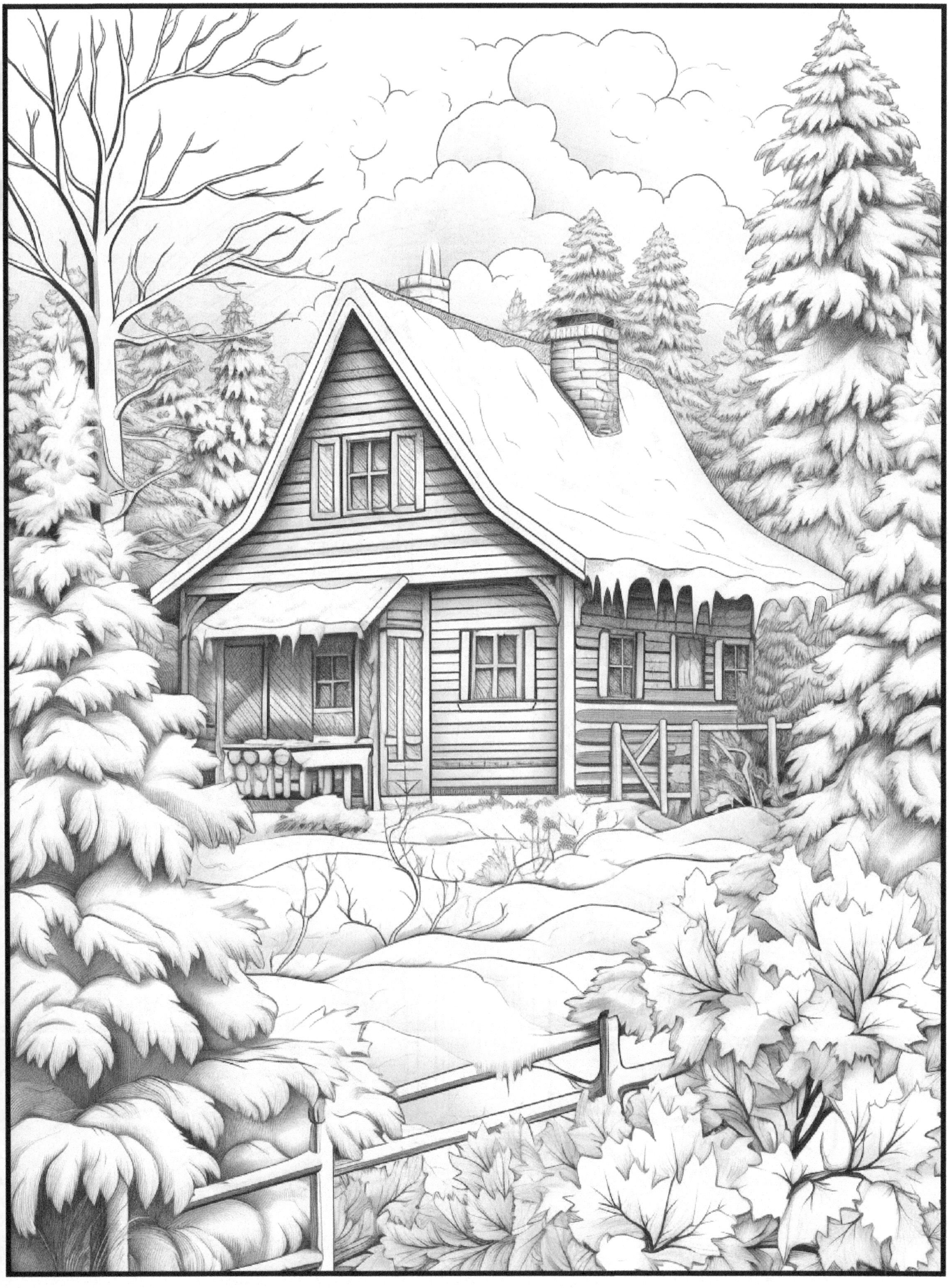

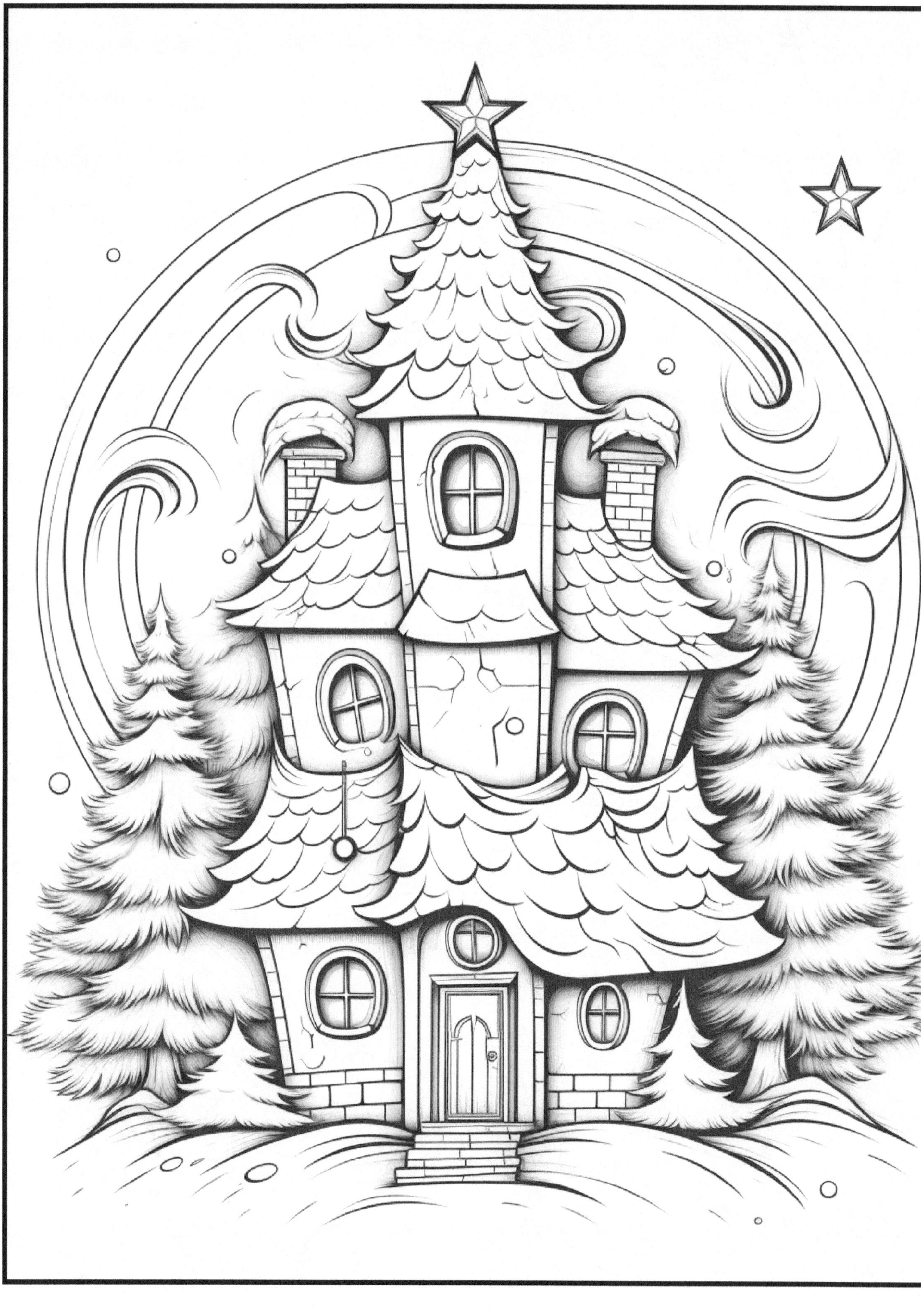

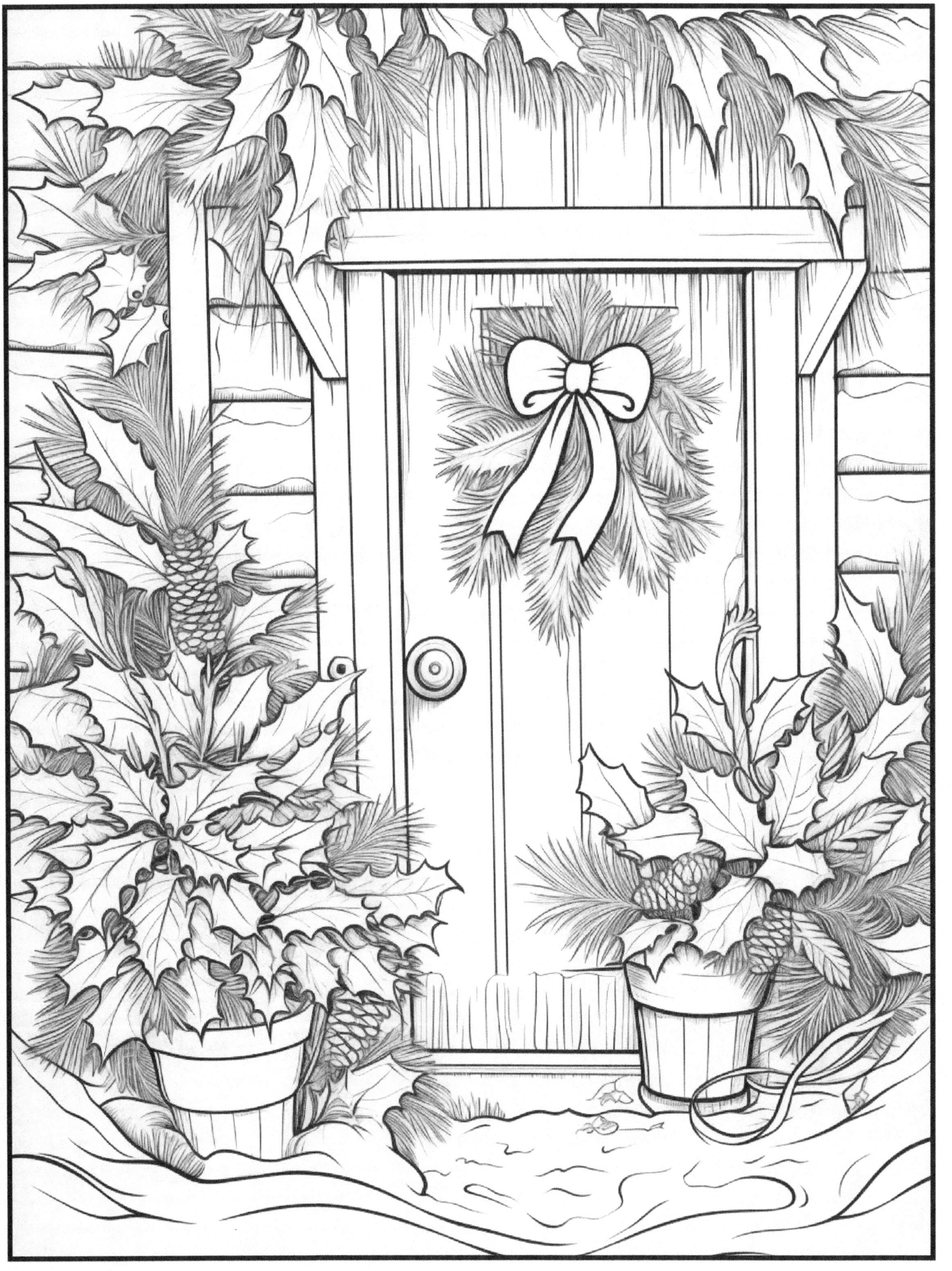

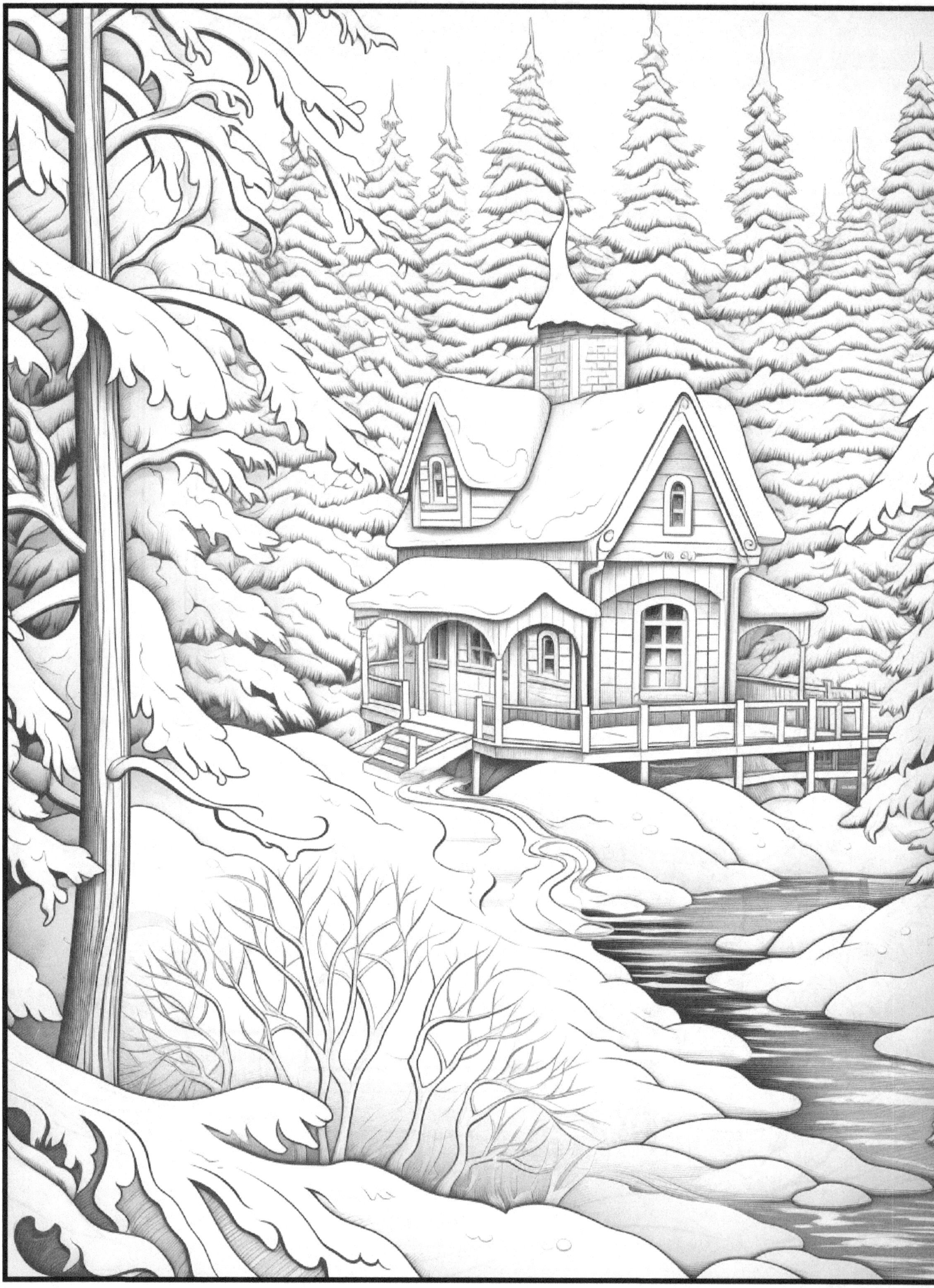

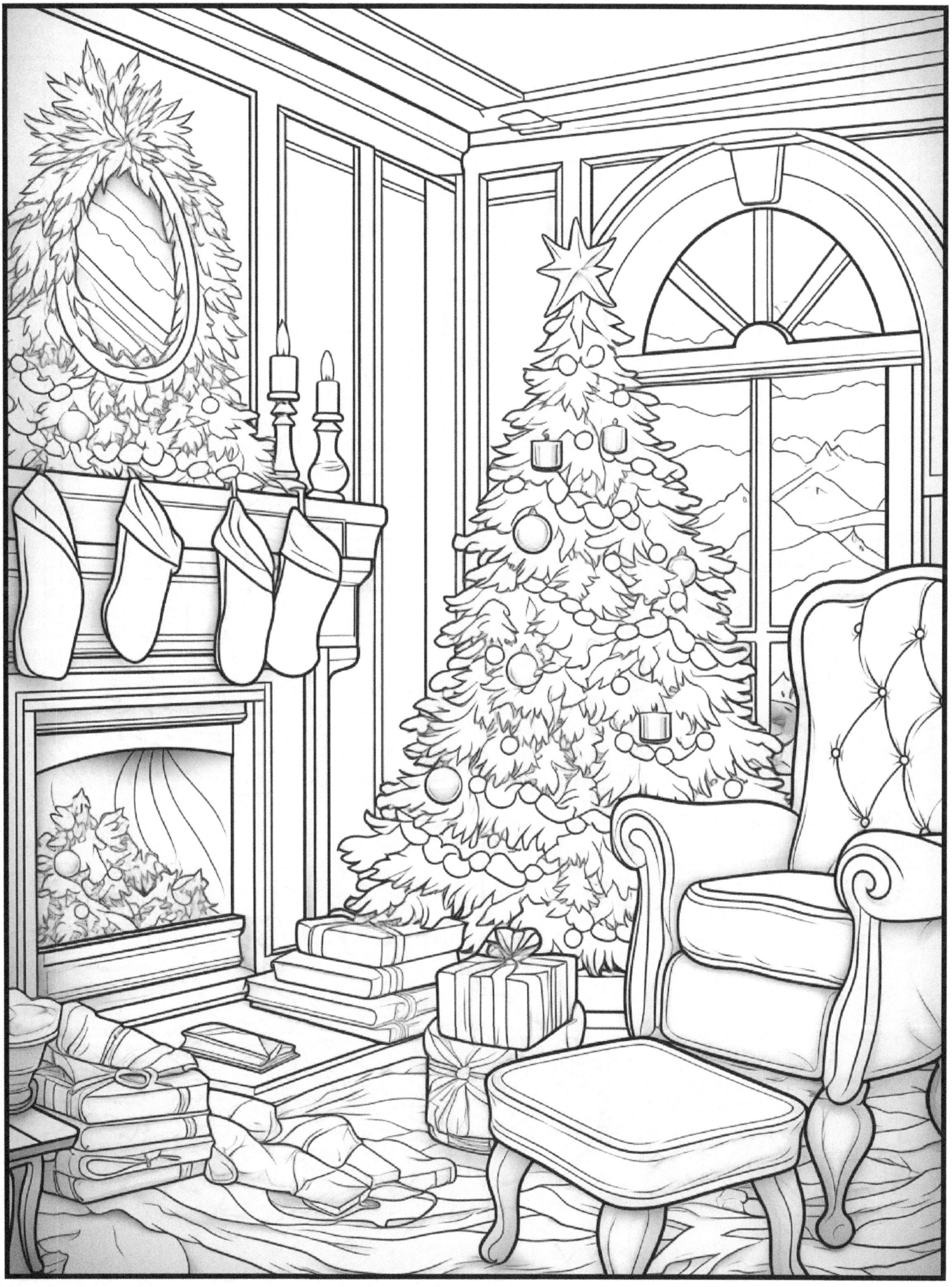

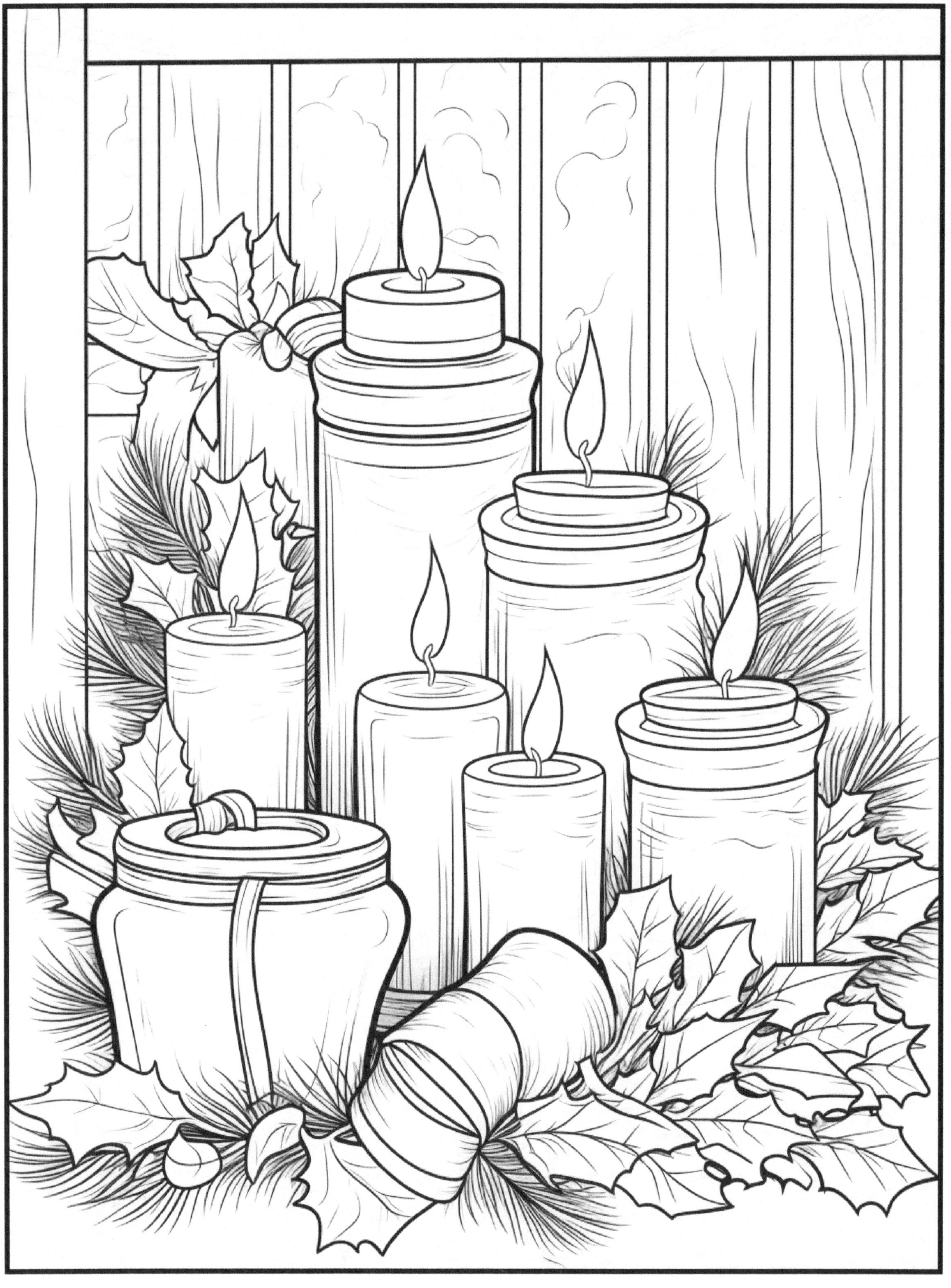

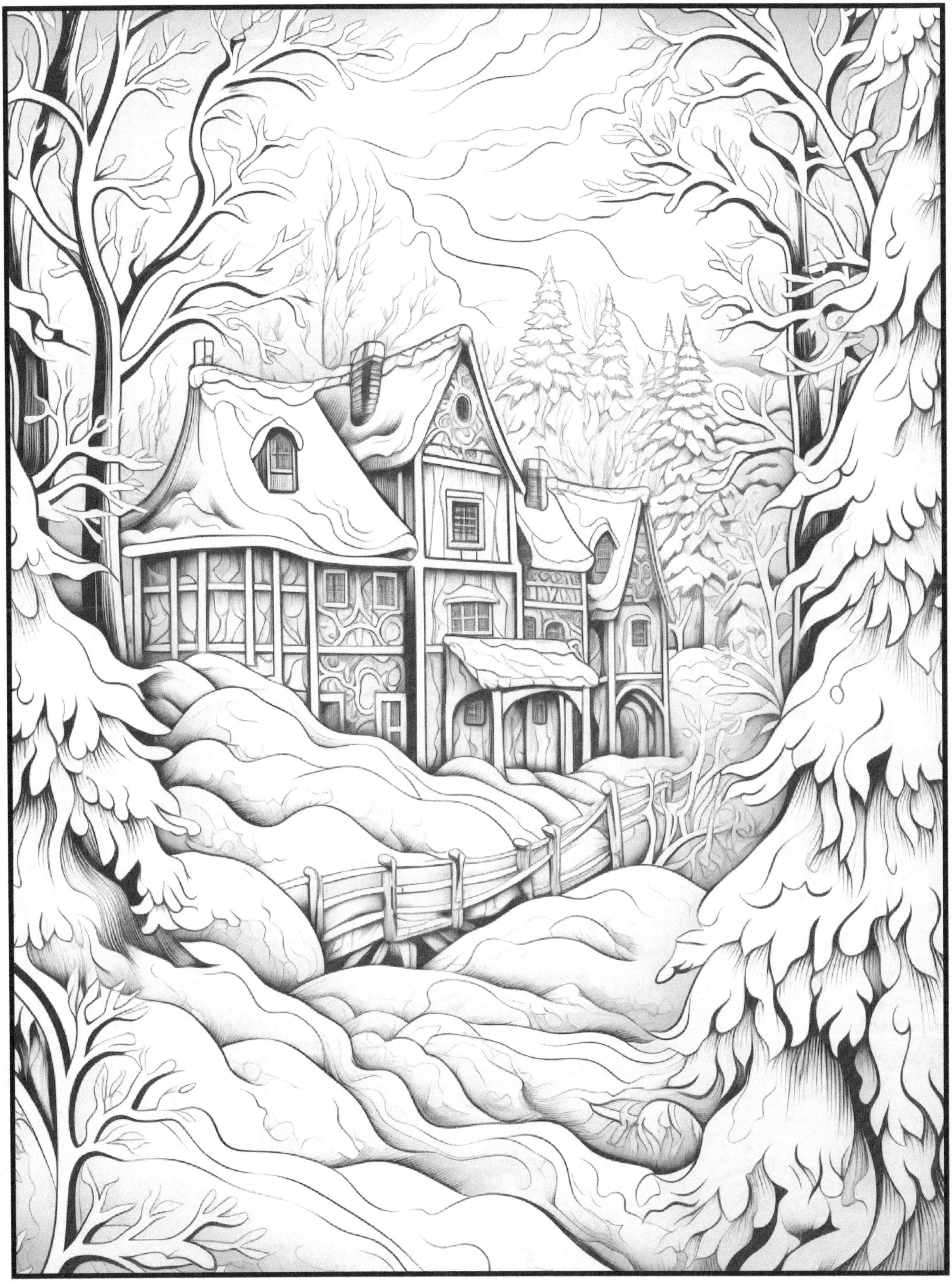

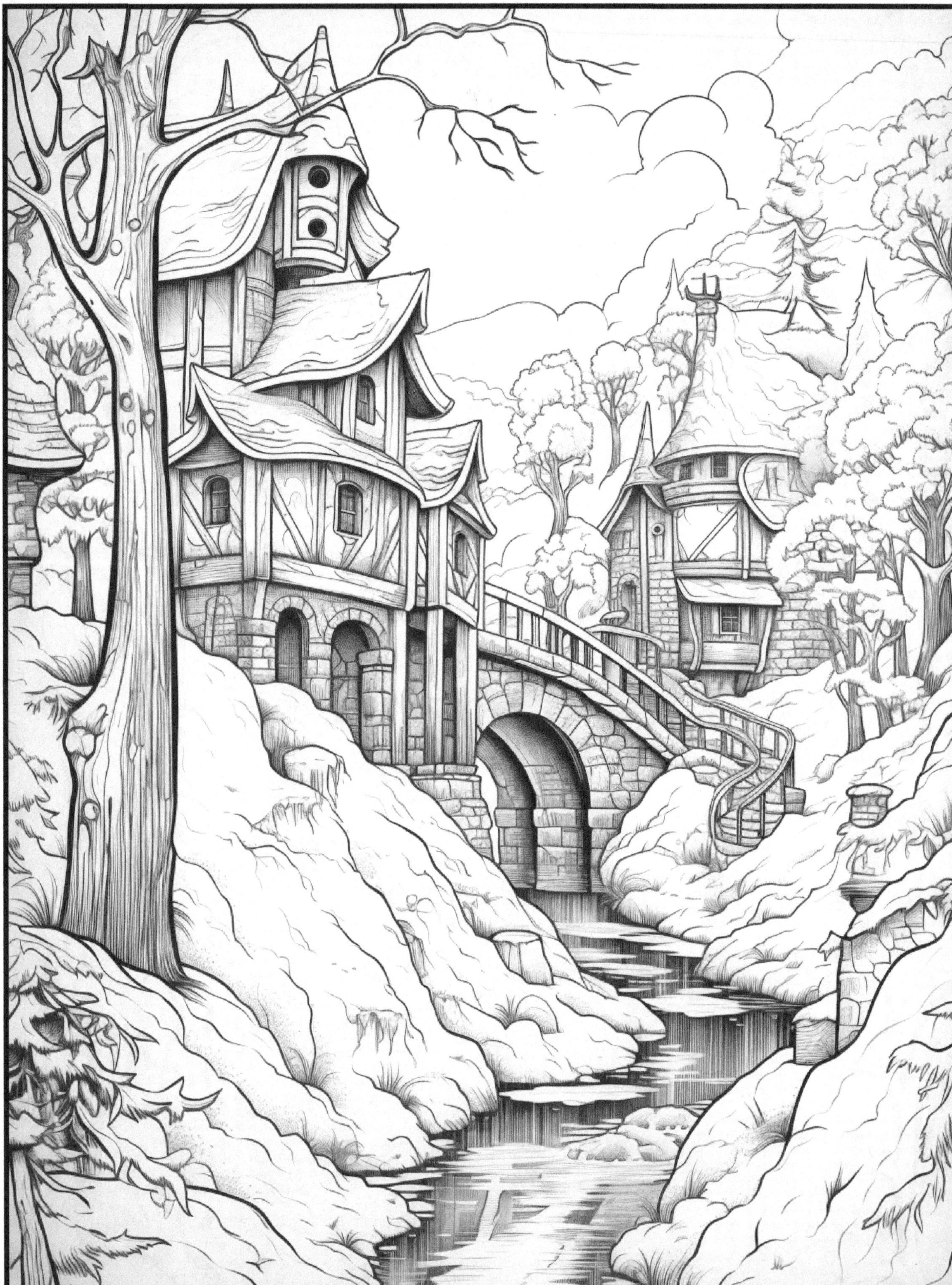

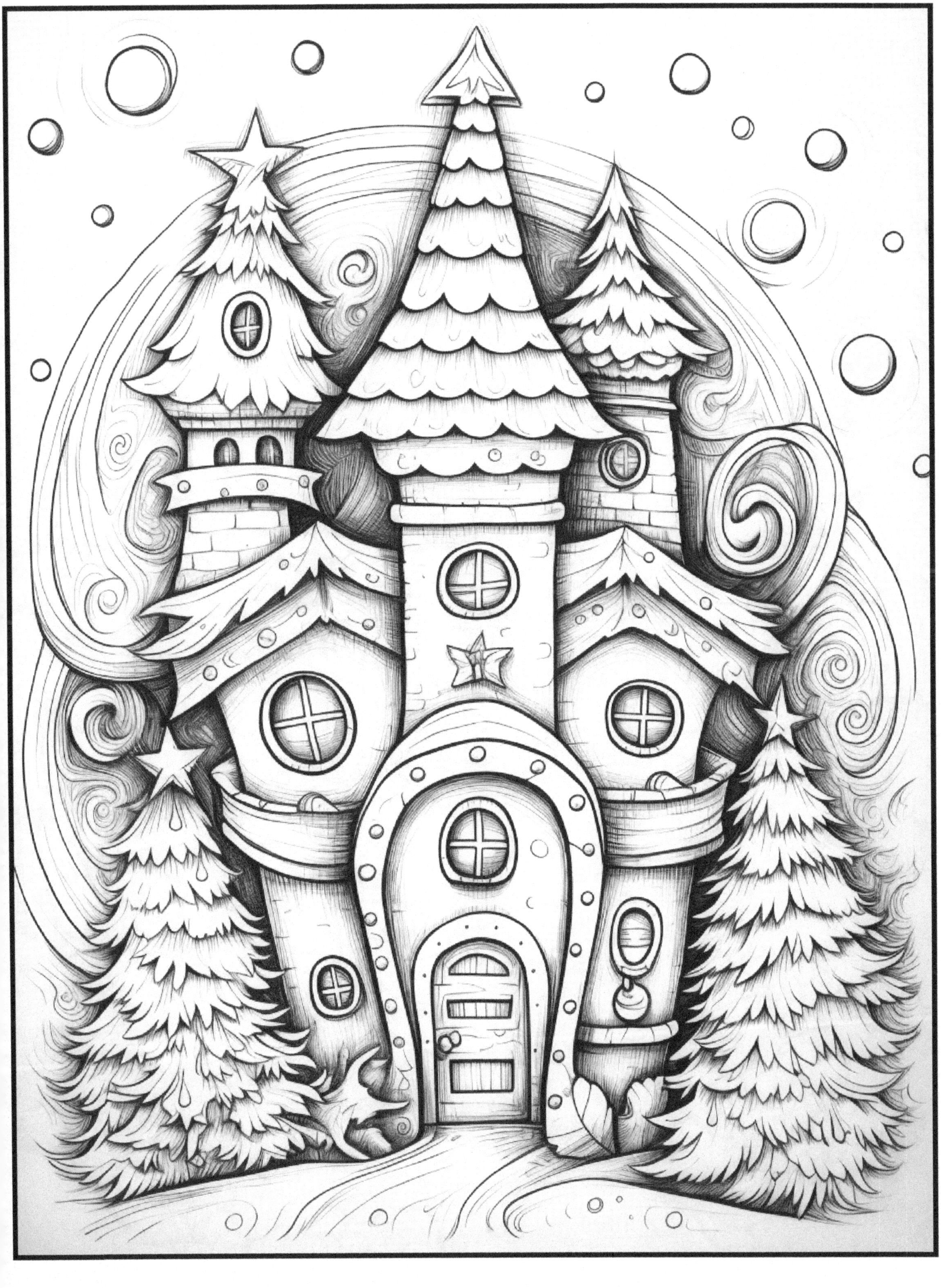

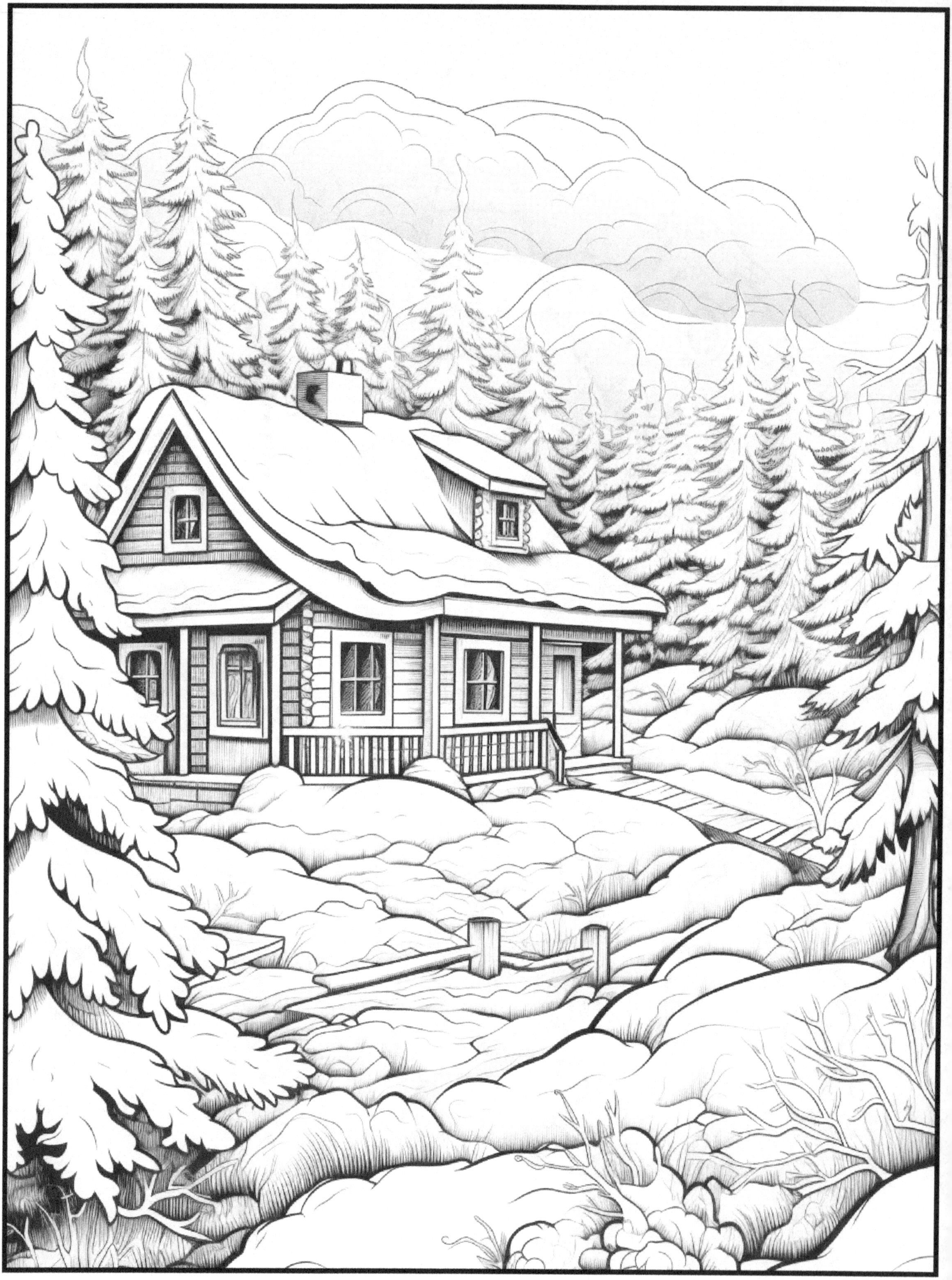

Made in the USA
Columbia, SC
17 December 2023

28864976R00037